The Compleat Pastor

THE COMPLEAT PASTOR

Minister, Leader, and Manager

DAVID J. CANTILLO, PhD

XULON PRESS

Xulon Press
2301 Lucien Way #415
Maitland, FL 32751
407.339.4217
www.xulonpress.com

© 2019 by David J. Cantillo, PhD

All rights reserved solely by the author. The author guarantees all contents are original and do not infringe upon the legal rights of any other person or work. No part of this book may be reproduced in any form without the permission of the author. The views expressed in this book are not necessarily those of the publisher.

Unless otherwise indicated, Scripture quotations taken from the King James Version (KJV)—*public domain*.

Printed in the United States of America.

ISBN-13: 978-1-5456-8072-8

Preface

The Compleat Angler is a book by Izaak Walton, first published in 1653, celebrating the art and spirit of fishing in prose and verse. It has become a classic of its genre, and generations of fisherman have enjoyed reading it. *The Compleat Angler* celebrates fishing as a way of life and the philosophy that can be gleaned from such a simple and enjoyable task.

This book and other writings by Izaak Walton have offered many thoughtful and provoking quotes, such as:

"No man can lose what he never had."

"The person that loses their conscience has nothing left worth keeping."

"God has two dwellings; one in heaven, and the other in a meek and thankful heart."

"I love such mirth as does not make friends ashamed to look upon one another next morning."

"God never did make a more calm, quiet, innocent recreation than angling."

"Good company in a journey makes the way seem shorter."

> "That which is everybody's business is nobody's business."

Coincidentally, Jesus called his followers fishers of men, and the most prominent of the disciples, Peter, was a fisherman before he became a fisher of men. *The Compleat Pastor* seeks to follow in both traditions, by offering a discourse on the art of pastoring (a way of life and a philosophy) for those called to be fishers of men.

Table of Contents

Preface v
My Personal Experience ix

Part 1: Principles

    Chapter 1: What a Pastor Does........................ 1
    Chapter 2: The Pastor as Minister.................... 19
    Chapter 3: The Pastor as Leader 33
    Chapter 4: The Pastor as Manager 47

Part 2: Further Applications

    MINISTRY 69
        Chapter 5: Assimilation, Discipleship, and Retention .. 71
        Chapter 6: Discipleship and Church Growth 87
    LEADERSHIP 99
        Chapter 7: Focus on the Leader 101
        Chapter 8: More on Leadership 115
    MANAGEMENT 131
        Chapter 9: Church Structure and Church Systems 133
        Chapter 10: Key Performance Indicators for
        Measuring Church Health........................... 147

Final Words 161
Appendix I – Sample Vision Statement................... 163
Appendix II – MBTI Types Descriptors................... 165
Appendix III – LVM for Five Choices 167
Appendix IV – Historical Church Growth................. 171
Endnotes 177

My Personal Experience
(Or why should you listen to anything I have to say)

What is my pastoral experience? I have been exposed to the job of pastoring from birth until the present. I grew up in a pastor's home, got an early view of the job, and decided I wanted no part of it. It took God more than thirty years to get me to the point that I was ready and willing to do the job. In the meantime, while living in various states, I was a church member under six different pastors. Finally, through the years, I have had close friendships with about five or six other pastors, and yes, I have been a pastor myself for over fifteen years. That's why I can say that I have been exposed to the pastoral life and work all my life, while at the same time pursuing my education in chemistry and counseling and working in industry and academia.

Enough about that... what about my personal experience as a pastor?

About thirteen years ago, our family and a small group pioneered the church I currently pastor in Florida. We began as a daughter church from an established congregation in Tampa. Through hard work and the grace of God, as I write, the church has grown to almost two hundred and fifty average in our Sunday morning attendance, and we have launched three other (still) small churches, with a total congregation (attendance based) around three fifty. In case you are good at math, there are two years of pastoral work missing—those I spent pastoring a small church up north.

After much reading, studying, and applying the principles I have learned, I think I understand the pathway from a small group to a congregation my size. My goal in sharing this book is to help pastors grow their churches from 30 to 300+. But the principles I will be sharing here are applicable to churches in the hundreds as well as the thousands.

In order to enhance the reader's ability to learn, I have referenced many sources of information, which will be found in the Endnotes section at the end of the book. I have personally studied and applied principles from those sources and have found that they are useful. My desire would be that the reader would consider this book as a starting point for further growth and research, and the references will help in that endeavor. In this sense, I invite the reader to join me as a student of the job of pastoring, not the world's expert on the subject.

Much information has been published about the role of the pastor in the local congregation. The goal of this book is to offer a *practical framework* for organizing that information, and some questions for *self-evaluation* and *development*. The desired end result is that the pastor may apply a few basic principles for personal growth and the growth of the church.

The premise of this work is easy to understand, and I have tried to present it in a simple way. **Part 1 – Principles** presents the basic ideas.

Part 2 – Further Applications goes deeper into some important concepts that apply to each of three areas of pastoral expertise. These can be implemented any time but would work best once the pastor has developed some proficiency in the areas of the job explained in the first part of the book.

How to Use this Book

My suggestion would be to carefully read chapters 1 through 4 and evaluate your expertise using the questions at the end of the chapters. Then go to any of the chapter areas (Ministry, chapters 5 and 6; Leadership, chapters 7 and 8; Management, chapters 9 and 10) as you feel the need to grow more specifically as a minister, leader, or manager.

PART 1: PRINCIPLES

This first section presents the basic principles of the job of the pastor in four chapters, with questions for reflection.

The main idea is that in a church with attendance/membership from 30–300+, a pastor needs to be:

- A minister with *anointing* to help people get saved and develop into disciples;
- A leader with *vision* to shape the strategy and goals for the church, and to motivate people to achieve those goals; and
- A manager with *wisdom* to establish structure and develop leadership for the functioning of the church.

Read on to understand each of these principles and to learn various ways to become effective and efficient at each of these jobs.

Note: Throughout the book I have used the male pronoun when referring to pastors, not meaning at all that a woman cannot be a pastor but being sensitive to the fact that the majority of pastors are men.

Note: All Scripture quotes are from the King James version of the Bible, unless otherwise stated.

Chapter 1: What a Pastor Does...

First Thoughts on Pastoral Work and Church Growth

Most pastors want their churches to grow larger. The Bible in various places refers to the church as the body of Christ, and we know that it is normal for a body to grow if it is healthy. Although there is a great deal of variation in the human body size, there is a normal amount of growth over the years on the way to adulthood. This principle applies to churches as well. After all, just about all pastors want their churches to grow!

When *normal* growth[1] is not reached, pastors try to find an explanation. Some may think that it is not God's will for that particular church or for the pastor's ministry to be any larger. However, as a general principle, churches should not remain small when there are millions needing salvation. Sometimes pastors blame the lack of growth on their preaching or teaching skills, but there are small churches pastored by great preachers and large churches pastored by preachers who are not as inspiring. The point here is that the growth of the church does not necessarily depend on God restricting growth or on the pastor's preaching, but on the work of the pastor *outside of the pulpit*.

There are many aspects of the pastor's work that form the foundation of a solid church: preaching biblical messages, the prayer life of the pastor, sound doctrine, holiness and separation to God, love for people, hard work, etc. Assuming those basic things are in place, there are many other things a pastor can do that will help the church to continue to grow through the years. Much of it has to do with the *role of the pastor* and the *structure* and *functioning* of the church (church systems). Although we will refer briefly to the structure and function of the church, this book will focus more on the role of the pastor.

Church Systems

The human body operates through *systems* to achieve the tasks necessary for life. For example, there is the respiratory system, the digestive system, the nervous system, and others. These systems are similar in all bodies, and when they function well, the body is healthy and it grows. The brain controls and monitors all of the body's systems constantly to maintain health.

The church is a spiritual body, and it also operates through systems that maintain its health. While Jesus is the head, in practice, the pastor is the director of the various church systems. His organization and supervision of the systems will impact their effectiveness, producing either growth or stagnation. We will look at church systems in a later chapter.

What Do Pastors Do?

For a starting point, the following verse from the book of Jeremiah presents God's point of view for what makes a good pastor:

> *Turn, O backsliding children, saith the LORD; for I am married unto you: and I will take you one of a city, and two of a family, and I will bring you to Zion:*

> *And I will give you pastors <u>according to mine heart</u>, which shall <u>feed</u> (pastor) you with <u>knowledge</u> and <u>understanding</u>. Jeremiah 3:14-15* [2]

The promise from the Lord is that He will establish pastors that will take care of His people according to His heart, with knowledge and understanding.

There are three different elements mentioned here that God wants in a pastor. The first is an understanding of the heart of God. A pastor must love God, be close to Him, and love people the same way God loves them. He must be a *minister* (servant) both to God and to the people, leading them closer to God.

Secondly, the pastor must feed or pastor the flock using knowledge. The most important thing a pastor needs to know is the will of God for himself and for the church. Paul prays for the Colossians that they may be filled with the "knowledge of his will" (Colossians 1.9). This can be defined as *vision*.

Finally, the pastor must use understanding as he pastors his church. Another word for understanding is *wisdom*. A pastor needs much wisdom to work effectively, organizing the work of the church to reach the lost and to promote spiritual growth in its members

What God Expects from Shepherds

In the book of Ezekiel, God speaks to the shepherds and complains that they have not done their job taking care of His sheep. He lists the following things:

> *Woe be to the shepherds of Israel that do feed themselves! should not the shepherds feed the flocks?*
>
> *Ye eat the fat, and ye clothe you with the wool, ye kill them that are fed: but ye feed not the flock.*

> *The diseased have ye not strengthened, neither have ye healed that which was sick, neither have ye bound up that which was broken, neither have ye brought again that which was driven away, neither have ye sought that which was lost; but with force and with cruelty have ye ruled them.*
>
> *And they were scattered, because there is no shepherd: and they became meat to all the beasts of the field, when they were scattered.*
>
> *My sheep wandered through all the mountains, and upon every high hill: yea, my flock was scattered upon all the face of the earth, and none did search or seek after them. Ezekiel 34:2-6*

We can look at this passage and turn the negative into a positive to understand what God expects from pastors. The list may be divided into three general areas: taking care of the needs of the sheep, guiding the sheep, and setting a vision for the care of the flock.

Taking care of the sheep can be likened to ministering to people (ministry). So, according to this Scripture, the pastor is responsible for feeding the flock, strengthening the diseased, healing the sick, and binding up the broken. This sounds like the ministry declaration of Jesus in Luke 4:18.

The shepherd is also responsible for guiding the sheep with kindness (management). So he should bring home those driven away, seek the lost, rule with gentleness and kindness, and, in general, gather the flock.

Finally, in contrast to a flock that is scattered throughout mountains and hills, God wants shepherds that have a vision of a flock that is protected and well cared for (leadership).

When a pastor fulfills these roles, he can be a complete pastor according to the desires and requirements of God as expressed by Jeremiah and Ezekiel.

Premise: The Work of the Pastor

There is much literature on effective church planting, but there has not been much written to help the church planter take the church from infancy into maturity. One key concept is that as the church grows through various stages, the *role of the pastor* and the *structure of the church* have to change.

Building on the discussion above, the pastor must be able to work as a minister, a leader, and a manager as the situation requires. Although these three jobs overlap in that they relate to the same group of people, the principles applied in each area are completely different. It is very different to work with someone as a minister and help them with their difficulties, and then work with the same person as a manager and move them in or out of a leadership position. When the pastor acts in a situation in the wrong role, he cannot be effective and may actually be counterproductive without realizing it. It is no wonder that pastoring is such a difficult job!

Jesus Our Pastor: Priest, Prophet, and King

Jesus refers to Himself as the good shepherd (John 10:11) who gives His life for His sheep. Peter refers to Jesus as the chief shepherd (1 Peter 2:25). A favorite Scripture to many, Psalm 23, emphasizes the role of God as our shepherd. Of course, the New Testament word for *shepherd* is *pastor*.

But there are three special terms that further describe the role of Jesus, our pastor: he is a priest, a prophet, and a king.

These three Old Testament terms are functionally equivalent to the three terms used above to describe the job of pastors today.

Priest = Minister
Prophet = Leader
King = Manager

Jesus functioned as a priest after the order of Melchizedek (Hebrews 6:20). He ministered in a tabernacle not made of hands but in the presence of God (Hebrews 9:11) and was both the priest and the sacrifice for our sins. 1 Timothy 2:5 clearly says that He is the mediator between God and man. The New Testament version of the priest is the *minister*.

Jesus referred to Himself as a prophet in various places (Luke 13:33; Matthew 13:57). In the book of Acts there are references to Jesus as a prophet (Acts 3:15, 22-23). A prophet is someone who reveals God and communicates His will to the people. Jesus shared a vision of a triumphant church, as He stated to Peter in Matthew 16:18. In all this, Jesus is functioning as a *leader*, presenting a vision and setting goals for His followers (Mark 16:15; Luke 24:49; Acts 1:8).

Scripture also refers to Jesus as the King of the Jews (Matthew 27:11 and 21:5), a title He accepted. But in the book of Revelations, He comes as the King of kings (Revelation 17:14 and 19:16). A king is a ruler that administers a nation, and we know that in the millennial reign, Jesus will be king of the whole earth. Thus, Jesus in this role is functioning as a *manager*.

As undershepherds to Jesus, our work also includes these three roles of the pastorate. This is another foundation to the principle that the work of the pastor involves being a minister, a leader, and a manager.

The Work of the Pastor: A Minister...

In a small church, the pastor works first as a minister, serving people directly by meeting their spiritual and material needs. In order to be effective in this function, the pastor needs *anointing*—to free people from the bondage of sin into the liberty of Christ. The pastor continues to minister to people, helping them to grow into mature disciples of Jesus. This work involves various things like preaching, teaching, and counseling. Each of these tasks is a little different, and more will be presented about them in the chapter on ministry. Most pastors can only directly minister to around seventy to one hundred people, which is why many churches stop growing when membership reaches those numbers.

The Work of the Pastor: A Leader...

To be successful in working with a larger congregation, the pastor must become an effective leader by presenting a clear and compelling *vision* before the church. He must help the congregation shift its motivation from a relationship with him (the pastor) to a commitment to a common vision. Together with church leadership, the pastor must present the vision in a compelling way, help craft a mission statement to clarify the direction, establish the strategy for its fulfillment, and develop short-term and long-terms goals.

The Work of the Pastor: A Manager...

In order to effectively mobilize resources and people for work, the pastor also functions as a manager. This is particularly important for a small/start-up church, since initially the pastor may have to do almost everything! However, even with a group as small as fifty, the pastor cannot realistically serve the needs of the entire congregation personally and also have time to plan for growth and take care of his own family. This becomes even more difficult for the bivocational pastor. Thus, the pastor must function as a manager, operating with *wisdom* in establishing the structure of the church, forming teams to accomplish tasks, appointing leaders for those teams, and organizing the work. The pastor needs to have some knowledge of the systems of the church so that instead of doing all the work himself, he can train and supervise others as they work.

John C. Maxwell advances the thought that as a pastor grows through time, he transitions from minister to leader to manager. He compares a minister to a shepherd, a leader to a rancher, and a manager to a foreman. While these comparisons are helpful, in a local church, the pastor has to transition back and forth among all three roles for his work to be effective and the church to grow.

Maxwell also has put forth a hierarchy of "levels of leadership" that detail the growth of a person to positions of greater influence. The five levels are: Position, Permission, Production, People Development, and Personhood.[3] But these levels are not all equally important for the development of the pastor. In a church, the pastor as a leader often begins work at the level of "Permission," where the people grant him the authority to be their pastor. The next important level is that of "People Development," where the congregants experience personal growth from following the pastor, and thus are willing to further support him. Finally, the level of "Personhood" is applicable to the pastor as he matures as a leader after years of service.

Gary McIntosh in *One Size Doesn't Fit All*[4] also states that as a church goes from small (50-200) to medium (200-400) to large (400+), the role of the pastor changes. In a small church, the pastor is viewed in a relational manner. In a medium church, he is perceived as being a great planner and in a large church, he is viewed as a great leader and visionary. Clearly, these descriptions fit the model of a pastor transitioning from a minister role to a manager role to a leadership role.

However, a key idea presented in this book is that these three functions need to be *present from the beginning* of the church in order for it to grow. Thus, there is a need for the pastor even of a small church to be proficient in all three areas if the church is to grow larger.

In a church with membership around three hundred and above, these three roles of minister, leader, and manager may be separated into different pastoral positions. There may be one pastor that works as the wise manager, a different pastor may be that charismatic leader that communicates vision, and various pastors may minister to the needs of the congregation. Understanding the necessity of these roles will still be helpful to the large church as pastoral staff are hired and developed.

The Pastor's Work Is Work!

A young man in my church once told me confidentially his idea of the work of the pastor. He thought the typical day of the pastor began around 9 or 10 am with a leisurely breakfast and reading of Scriptures. It progressed to a calm review of church matters, leading into lunch, a nap afterwards perhaps, and then a long afternoon of more Bible study and reflection. In the evening, before the wife served dinner, possibly some phone calls to church members and maybe a home visit afterwards.

This daily schedule would get repeated weekdays, except for Sundays. On Sundays, a great sermon, product of all those Bible studies, would be expounded to the congregation for their amazement and approval. Of course, this life would get supported by the unfailing and consistent generosity of the saints!

Based on this understanding of the pastoral life, this young man had a desire to become a pastor as soon as possible.

However, as he began to work with me and to see the actual work of the pastorate, his thinking changed! Later he stated that if the Lord calls him to pastoral work, he would be willing to do it, but he is perfectly happy just assisting the pastor for now. This young man has become a fine assistant to me personally and to the church. With a few more years of maturity under his belt, he may make a good pastor now that he has a real understanding of the work involved.

The real work of the pastor does not include concepts like "leisurely breakfast," "calm reviews," naps, and lots of Bible study time. It is more like early prayer amid hustle and bustle, crisis management, hurried sermon preparation, and always a time crunch. Dinner is not always served, but may be microwaved as needed, and home visits may occur at any time in the twenty-four-hour day. Oh, and the salary of the average pastor is a work in progress, although the retirement package is out of this world!

Why would anyone consider being a pastor then? The answer is *a calling from God*. That should be the sole reason for moving in that direction.

The work of the pastor is endless, and perhaps more perspiration than inspiration. Of course, there are great blessings and rewards from God, material and spiritual. But as we consider this calling, let this serve as warning that the work of the pastor is a lot of *work*.

Paul described the work of a church planter in even starker terms:

> *Are they ministers of Christ? (I speak as a fool) I am more; in labours more abundant, in stripes above measure, in prisons more frequent, in*

Chapter 1: What a Pastor Does...

deaths oft. Of the Jews five times received I forty stripes save one.

Thrice was I beaten with rods, once was I stoned, thrice I suffered shipwreck, a night and a day I have been in the deep;

In journeyings often, in perils of waters, in perils of robbers, in perils by mine own countrymen, in perils by the heathen, in perils in the city, in perils in the wilderness, in perils in the sea, in perils among false brethren; In weariness and painfulness, in watchings often, in hunger and thirst, in fastings often, in cold and nakedness.

Beside those things that are without, that which cometh upon me daily, the care of all the churches.

Who is weak, and I am not weak? who is offended, and I burn not? If I must needs glory, I will glory of the things which concern mine infirmities.

The God and Father of our Lord Jesus Christ, which is blessed for evermore, knoweth that I lie not.

In Damascus the governor under Aretas the king kept the city of the Damascenes with a garrison, desirous to apprehend me: And through a window in a basket was I let down by the wall, and escaped his hands. 2 Corinthians 11:23-33

Thank you, my brother Paul. Compared to your experience, the busiest pastoral life today seems like a walk in the park. It may not be an easy life like some innocently think, but for the most part, it is not like Paul's experience. It is a good life, a worthy life, if you are called. There is no higher vocation this side of heaven.

The Pastor's Call

Any person called to serve God (pastor, prophet, or apostle) needs to feel a definite and clear call from God to do that kind of work. Albeit, the call may come in different manners, as seen by some Bible characters. Samuel received a direct, supernatural communication from God that set him on the path to be a special prophet to God's people. However, Elisha and Isaiah were called in a different manner. Elijah cast his mantle over Elisha, and he followed Elijah as master, serving him in all things until the end when he asked for a double portion of the spirit. Isaiah had a vision of heaven when a call went out, "Whom shall I send, and who will go for us?" Isaiah volunteered, "Here am I, send me."

In the same manner, the effect of the call on each life may be different. At first, there is a thrilling response of the soul to the knowledge that we have been called to serve God Almighty. But on the way to the fulfillment of that call, there will be trials and adversity. Noah was called of God and preached 120 years, and no one got saved except his own family. Jeremiah was called of God to preach to a rebellious people and suffered greatly at their hands, even though he preached the truth to them. Peter was thrown in jail for preaching, and only an angel's miraculous intervention saved his life. Stephen was martyred for preaching the gospel, and Paul was initially rejected by the Jews, and later, persecuted by Gentiles while doing the will of God and planting churches all over Asia Minor.

The pastor today is a spiritual descendant of the Old Testament prophets and the New Testament apostles. We must receive a clear call although it may come in different manners. Just like them, while doing the work, we may face persecution and adversity, even though we may be doing the will of God. But a real call from God will get ahold of our souls and not let go until we fulfill it. Paul said it this way:

> ... but I follow after, if that I may apprehend that for which also I am apprehended of Christ Jesus. Phil. 3:12

To conclude this chapter, let's look again at the three aspects of the pastor's work:

- A minister with *anointing* to help people get saved and develop as disciples;
- A leader with *vision* to shape the strategy and goals for the church, and to motivate people to achieve those goals and
- A manager with *wisdom* to establish structure and develop leadership for the functioning of the church.

Based on my experience as a lifelong church member and now a pastor, I can state that most pastors function well as ministers but are not so effective in the leader and manager functions. Many are not aware of the distinction in those roles and struggle in managing the work of the congregation. This situation is complicated by the fact that the concepts used by a leader and a manager are very different from those of a minister. For example, the leader is looking toward the future, while the manager is concerned with the here and now.

The pastor has to learn to wear different hats at different times until the church grows to such a size that it can support different pastors for different roles. For the visual learners, one could envision those hats to be: the *minister* wearing the miter of the Old Testament priest, the *leader* sporting a cowboy hat, and the *manager* wearing a baseball cap.

In the following chapters, we will delve in detail into each of these roles for the pastor, with resources for further reading and questions for personal evaluation and development.

To consider the differences, the following page has a chart comparing the work of the minister, manager, and leader, modified from a John Maxwell seminar.

Ministry, Management, and Leadership

Comparison

Ministry: Serving God by helping others through personal gifting.

Management: Serving God by organizing teams to accomplish godly goals.

Leadership: Serving God by casting vision for the church and motivating teams.

Chapter 1: What a Pastor Does...

Ministry – Shepherd	Management – Foreman	Leadership – Rancher
Adds	Applies	Multiplies
Responds to people	Coaches others to create	Envisions future
Concentrates on lower 20%	Moves lower 60% to upper 20%	Concentrates on upper 20%
Motivated by needs	Motivated by accomplishment	Motivated by vision
Finds task fulfilling	Finds organized work fulfilling	Finds vision casting fulfilling
Retains people	Coordinates people	Releases people
Works short term	Works short term and long term	Works long term
Maintains	Organizes	Grows
Stability oriented	Results oriented	Change oriented
Counselor	Coach	Developer
Lives by demands	Lives by goals	Lives by purpose
Thinks short term	Connects short term to long term	Thinks long term

Adapted from John Maxwell: "The Difference Between Ministry and Leadership."

Case Study: Ministry or Management?

Joe is a 35-year old church member, married, with two small children. He is a team leader for a construction company specializing in remodeling. He and his wife were baptized three years ago and have been faithfully attending church. Joe struggles with a secret pornography addiction, and the pastor has been counseling him over the past six months. He has made some progress, but still is often tempted, particularly due to his friends at work. Although his wife is unaware of this situation, it has affected the marriage relationship, and she feels something is not quite right. Joe and his wife have a desire to serve God and be involved in the church.

What does the pastor do?

As a minister, he counsels Joe to help him overcome his addiction. He prays for him daily; they talk on the phone at least once a week to keep in touch and they meet once every two weeks. He prays for Joe specifically during church services and ministers deliverance from the spiritual aspect of his addiction.

As a wise manager, the pastor asks Joe to join the new building maintenance group under the guidance of an older saint. Joe has a lot of knowledge that can help with the work, and it is good for him to get involved in service. Being around a mature Christian helps him to have a clear model of where he needs to be in Christ.

However, if the pastor confuses the minister and manager roles, he may place Joe in charge of the new building maintenance group to try to help him shift his focus from his problem to the church service, even though his spiritual life is not quite ready for this. Joe is qualified for that leadership role on the basis of his secular job, but taking a leadership role in a church group would be harmful to him and to the other saints that may perceive some problems in Joe's spiritual life.

Likewise, if the pastor confuses his minister and leader roles, he may ask Joe to preach at the next youth service, even though Joe is not ready to minister. The pastor may do this because he sees such potential in Joe (vision) and wants to move him forward into that potential.

It would be more appropriate to continue with counseling until Joe has overcome his addiction for some time and is ready to move into a mentoring relationship for further growth. The way the pastor handles Joe's situation is crucial for his spiritual growth and for his future service to the church. Because the pastor is a caring minister, Joe may be saved, but his utility to God's kingdom may be damaged by the wrong approach. On the other hand, a relationship with a pastor who knows about management and leadership will actually help to develop Joe's talents so that, over time, all of his skills may be used for God's kingdom.

Questions

1. Do you as a pastor understand the three functions of the pastor explained here? How would you evaluate yourself as a minister, leader, and manager? Rate yourself on a scale of 1–5, with 5 being maximum.

Minister	1	2	3	4	5
Leader	1	2	3	4	5
Manager	1	2	3	4	5

2. Can you remember some instances where you succeeded or failed at either the leader or manager functions as described above? What can you learn now, reflecting on your previous experience?

3. Based on your self-analysis in question 1, which of the three areas do you most need to develop in yourself? Do you have specific steps you can take in the next three months? If not, that's ok. Read on…

Chapter 2: The Pastor as Minister

Who Is a Minister?

A minister is someone that has a special relationship with God concerning a calling to do a particular work. All Christians are called to ministry (service), but there is also a special calling upon some to be the voice of God, to lead others and to shepherd a congregation. There are several types of ministry, but here we are focusing on the pastoral ministry, which has two aspects, ministry to God and ministry to the people.

In the book of Ezekiel, the writer makes a difference between two types of ministers as a result of their faithfulness to God.

> *And the Levites that are gone away far from me, when Israel went astray, which went astray away from me after their idols; they shall even bear their iniquity.*
>
> *Yet they shall be ministers in my sanctuary, having charge at the gates of the house, and ministering to the house: they shall <u>slay the burnt offering and the sacrifice for the people</u>, and they shall stand before them to <u>minister unto them</u>. Ezekiel 44:10-11*

> *But the priests the Levites, the sons of Zadok, that kept the charge of my sanctuary when the children of Israel went astray from me, they shall come near to me to <u>minister unto me</u>, and they shall stand before me <u>to offer unto me the fat and the blood</u>, saith the Lord GOD:*
>
> *They shall enter into my sanctuary, and they shall <u>come near to my table</u>, to minister unto me, and they shall keep my charge. Ezekiel 44:15-16*

The first group of Levites was given a specific task to minister to the people and take care of the outward process of the sacrifice at the gates of the house. Their job was to prepare the sacrifice before the people so that they could come as close to God as the gates of the tabernacle. Because of their sin, they could not draw near to God themselves, but they could serve the people.

The second group of Levites had the job of offering to God the inward parts of the sacrifice and to stand near the table of the Lord in the Holy Place. The table is probably a reference to the table of shewbread, where the priests had the job of eating some of the bread in the presence of the Lord. These are people that have the privilege of drawing near to God and participating in His glory. They had this special place because they were faithful.

Both of these functions, *ministering to God* and *ministering to the people*, are required of the New Testament priests, the ministers. Thus, the first job of the pastor as a minister is to draw near to God and have a close relationship with Him. The second job is serving the people and helping them draw near to God. Unfortunately, due to the busyness of the second job, the first job is often neglected. This is tragic, because a fruitful ministry cannot occur without time spent close to God. A minister cannot guide people any closer to God than the place where he is *himself* in that relationship.

The Minister as a Servant

The New Testament defines the minister (*diakonia*) as a servant, which focuses his work on being attentive to the desires of the person being served. The New Testament minister serves God first, not the people, by seeking and doing the will of God in the church. The specific work is praying, preaching, teaching, counseling, and coaching (mentoring). The minister draws closer to God for personal edification and direction, and then communicates what he receives from the Lord to the people.

The goal of the pastor as a minister in regard to the congregation is to meet the needs of the people and also to train the people for reproducing the pastor's ministry into other lives. The Bible puts it this way in Ephesians; we call it the five-fold ministry:

And he gave some, apostles; and some, prophets; and some, evangelists; and some, pastors and teachers; For the perfecting of the saints, for the work of the ministry, for the edifying of the body of Christ:

Till we all come in the unity of the faith, and of the knowledge of the Son of God, unto a perfect man, unto the measure of the stature of the fulness of Christ: Ephesians 4:11-13

Although this text also deals with vision (stature of fullness of Christ) and management (edifying the body), the focus of the work of the five-fold ministry is perfecting believers and helping them to grow spiritually (ministry).

A Word on Anointing

Ok, lots of words... Anointing is a hard thing to define, sort of like beauty. Philosophers have debated on the nature of beauty. One wrote a book on *The Sense of Beauty* and concluded by saying, "Beauty is a pledge of the possible conformity between the soul and nature, and consequently a ground of faith in the supremacy of the good."[5] To put it in plain English, "Beauty is in the eye of the beholder." I would propose that anointing is known in the spirit of the hearer, meaning that one can perceive an anointed message or life when exposed to it, but we have a hard time defining it apart from the experience itself.

The word *anointing* is first used in the Bible in reference to the oil that was to be used only to consecrate the vessels of the Tabernacle and the priests for service. The oil was poured over the item to be consecrated, and from there on, it was *anointed*, or used only for God's service. Although various Hebrew words were used for anointing, the meaning stayed the same: the application of sacred oil to an object or person. The only exception comes in Isaiah 10:27, where the anointing is used to bring liberty to the people of God, and it is evident that the meaning is a spiritual one.

In the New Testament, the word *anointing* is used to denote the power of God acting to heal a person (James 5:14) or to teach truth (1 John 2:27). Thus it can be likened to another New Testament grace (*charis*), which is defined as God's inward influence on a life.[6] The way we use the word *anointing* today is to refer to the distribution of grace to others through a consecrated person, a minister set aside for God's service.

An anointed minister, then, is a person who can influence others directly to salvation and a closer walk with God. Many people confuse the anointing with emotion, particularly among Pentecostal believers. Although most respond with emotion to the anointing, there are times when the anointing is operating even though there is not an emotional response.

In conclusion, the anointing of a minister may be judged by the result on the lives of others. It translates into people that are converted from a life of sin into a new life as children of God. Regardless of the manner of speaking or the actions, the anointed minister walks with God's grace and moves in the shadow of the Holy Spirit.

More Anointing?

The only way to have greater anointing is to live a life of spiritual discipline.

Many people dislike the word "discipline" because they associate it with things they were forced to do by authority figures like parents. Parents "made us" practice disciplines like brushing our teeth, taking regular showers or baths, or wearing clean clothes. These things we may have resisted while we were young, not knowing the value of their practice until we ourselves became adults. The ability to chew our food with our own teeth would have deteriorated long before we understood the value of brushing our teeth. Thank God for parents that forced us to that unpleasant task and taught us discipline in the small things! Unfortunately, a negative reaction to "discipline" may remain with us, although those disciplines we learned as children now bring health, wellness, and order to our complicated lives.

In our walk with God, spiritual disciplines keep us saved and help us to grow into mature Christians that can serve God and help others. We need to put away any negative reactions to the word *discipline* itself and embrace our spiritual disciplines as necessary and even enjoyable. Possibly the first time you heard of some of these, some spiritual "parent" was warning you that you needed to establish a practice of something like daily prayer and Scripture reading. Like a child, you may have questioned the necessity of such things. However, just as we see in the natural world, the value of our spiritual disciplines is understood only after we become spiritual adults. In fact, we may never become spiritual adults unless we practice spiritual disciplines!

Spiritual disciplines include things like daily prayer, real worship, giving of our resources, and the perspective of selflessness.[7] Consistent practice of these disciplines and others will craft a vessel that will hold greater anointing and be able to influence more people to a life of righteousness. Ministers can grow in their anointing and also lose their anointing due to a lack of these disciplines or due to unrepented sin.

Pastors should pray for anointing every day, confident that God will answer according to His riches in glory.

The Work of the Minister

What exactly is the work of ministers? The following paragraphs outline the most important activities that a minister must do to serve God and the people.

Praying

The minister must have a close relationship with God and be assured of his calling in order to be effective. This only comes through consistent, fervent prayer. A large part of the minister's prayer should be devoted to receiving direction from God. Rather than asking God to bless what the minister desires to do, he should strive to do what God does, knowing that it will be blessed. Jesus stated that the Son can do nothing of Himself, *but what he seeth the Father do: for what things soever he doeth, these also doeth the Son likewise.* (John 5:19). Truly, we cannot do anything on our own, but if we do what we see God doing, then we will be successful as ministers. If it was necessary for Jesus, it must be even more necessary for us.

The work of prayer accomplishes more in a church than any action of the minister. This is a hard thing for ministers to understand. Motivated by a desire to help, we believe that our words and action can change lives—what a mistake! Only Jesus can change a life. I have found that more change happens when I pray for people than when I talk to them about their problems. The hidden work of the minister in prayer will produce results beyond anything that he can humanly accomplish. All the wisdom and expertise in the world cannot substitute for one moment of grace! Jesus said it this way:

> *But thou, when thou prayest, enter into thy closet, and when thou hast shut thy door, pray to thy Father which is in secret; and thy Father which seeth in secret shall reward thee openly.*
> *Matthew 6:6*

There are various models of prayer—praying through the Lord's Prayer (Matthew 6:9-13), putting on the armor of God (Ephesians 6:13-17), intercessory prayer—and the pastor should be cognizant of all of them and practice them. In any church, a vibrant prayer ministry is the motor that drives all the other activities toward success. Among prayer activities in the church, the pastor and his family should be leaders in praying regularly and encouraging prayer in the congregation.

Preaching

Preaching brings conviction through the word of God to people. It is aimed to reach the heart and cause a decision that will change the person. Preaching is both an art and a science in that the preacher must prepare in a systematic manner, but the delivery and inspiration are dependent on many factors, including the life of the preacher and, of course, the Holy Spirit.

The effectiveness of preaching depends on the prayer life of the minister and on his personal testimony before the people. The preacher must be a product of the message so that the congregation can see an example of the end result. Sermon preparation ought to begin with prayer, asking God what He wants to say to the people on that occasion. Anointing comes during the preparation as well as during the delivery of the message and its presence is not proven by the immediate response of the people but by the change in their lives.

There are many different ways to prepare and deliver sermons, as any homiletics course will show. Verbal Bean classified sermons into five categories: salvation, worship, consecration, exhortation, and encouragement.[8] However you may want to style your preaching, this is a very important part of the work of a minister, since God has chosen to save the lost by the foolishness of preaching (1 Corinthians 1:21).

All sermons follow a certain order, which has been found to work best for the culture and times. In our churches, most sermons begin with an introduction to capture the interest of the people, a body where themes, illustrations, and testimonies are presented, and a closing with a call to prayer at the altar. Sermons should have a scriptural foundation and draw people to the altar to get closer to God, be filled with the Holy Spirit, or receive a miracle.

Teaching

Teaching provides instruction to the people based on the Bible. It aims to inform the mind and provide direction for decisions. We need teaching in the church in order to make disciples. Jesus ordered His followers to *Go ye therefore, and teach all nations* (Matthew 28:19). God is so concerned with instruction that He gave us a very lengthy and detailed book (the Bible) with more information than we could ever digest in a lifetime!

There is a great need today for biblical teaching that comes from a love of the word of God and reaches the heart. Jesus was a master teacher in that He used simple stories and illustrations to drive home unforgettable truths. Without teaching, a church develops a shallow Christian life subject to every wind of doctrine and church fad that comes along.

In order to be an effective teacher, the minister must be a lifetime student! He should always be reading and studying, taking classes that will increase his knowledge and perspective concerning the work of the Lord. Ministers need to be aware of social and political trends, the culture and demographics of their areas, church growth factors, and pastoral development tips. Intellectual and spiritual isolation brings stagnation. There are many resources available today, both through personal associations in the fellowship and through books and seminars, that can be useful for growth.

Every minister should have a teaching plan to bring new converts from birth to adulthood to leadership. This includes Sunday school materials, Bible studies, and discipleship classes. If the teaching program of the church is not clearly laid out for new converts, they will develop haphazardly. Our educational system illustrates how a good teaching curriculum is implemented. There is a clear progression from what students get in first grade to the high school curriculum and beyond. All along, there are tests and outcome measures that institutions use to evaluate the growth of students. In the same way, spiritual growth must be directed. It does not happen automatically but results from experiences and instruction that shape a committed disciple of Jesus Christ. Tests will happen in the life of the believers, and the results will tell where they are in their spiritual growth.

Every pastor should have a clear progression of studies for new believers to shape their spiritual development. It can be unique classes developed in-house, published Bible studies, online courses, workshops, and retreats. There is some discussion of the process of discipleship in a later chapter.

Counseling

Ministry to the people also occurs when the pastor relates personally to someone, giving counsel regarding issues they are facing. Understanding how the human mind works and something about personality helps the pastor to understand people.

Pastoral counseling is an important part of the work of the minister. All counseling is based on a psychological theory of personality, even if the pastor is not aware of the principles. Ideas of subconscious motivations, for example, abound in our conversation and thoughts, and these originate in the theories of Sigmund Freud and Karl Jung, not in the Bible.

Some psychological principles are not aligned with the word of God, and some actually work against Christian doctrines. Well-meaning ministers sometime counsel people in the wrong direction based on ideas promoted by popular psychology or the plethora of self-help books available. Often these worldly ideas are combined with a short Scripture to make them palatable to Christians, and some fall into such practices without knowing the error.

For example, I have heard speakers say that we need to "love ourselves," because Jesus said that we have to love our neighbor as ourselves (Matthew 22:39). The argument is that if we don't love ourselves, we won't be able to love our neighbor. This type of sophistry turns Jesus' teaching completely backwards. He was teaching about loving others, which the Bible emphasizes in other verses, going so far as to say that we should esteem others better than ourselves (Philippians 2:3). The focus is not on self-love but on love for others.

Although formally trained as a counselor, I prefer not to engage in deep or lengthy counseling with church members. Such a practice actually falls into what counselors call a *dual relationship*, which is considered unhealthy for both parties. The dual relationship occurs because the same two people have both a counseling relationship and a pastoral relationship. Knowing too much about a church member can have a negative effect both on the person and the pastor. For that reason and others, any counseling I provide to my church members is short term and usually focused on one or two goals. For more intensive counseling needs, I refer to an outside counselor whom I can trust.

A minister should be prepared to offer counseling during major life events such as marriage (pre-marital and marriage therapy), the growth of children, and death in the family. Counseling on family issues can help families with children bring up healthy young Christians. Finally, understanding the grieving process and how it impacts peoples' lives will make any pastor more effective in providing support and guidance through difficult times.

A word of caution: while one may use techniques and theories from psychology to understand a particular situation, it is the power of God working through the Holy Spirit that heals and restores a person. Whether dealing with substance abuse, finances, or a marital problem, God has the answer and the power to change people from the inside out. The church continues the ministry of Jesus, as He declared in Luke 4:18, *to heal the brokenhearted, preach deliverance to captives and free them that are bruised.*

The most common mistake pastors make is to think that counseling is telling people what they need to do. This is wrong for two reasons. First, if the minister tells someone what to do and they do it and it works, then the believer may give the glory to the minister and not to God. This means that they will be back more and more to get direction in their lives instead of seeking it from the Lord on their own. On the other hand, if the person does what the minister says and it does not work, they will place the blame on the minister. Neither outcome is desirable!

Therefore, it is best to proceed with counseling by asking questions. It may be done, for example, by having the believer read something from the Scripture and then asking them, based on what they read, what they ought to do. That way, the counselee takes responsibility for learning from the word of God and obeying it. The pastor counselor is just a helper that is facilitating that process.

Coaching and Mentoring

Counseling helps people overcome their problems, but another form of guidance occurs when the pastor coaches and mentors people to help them develop and mature. This type of relationship is interested in helping people grow in achieving tasks (coaching) and in overall personal growth (mentoring).

The pastor becomes a coach when he helps people practice some of the things that he has been teaching them. This is a relatively short-term relationship that is focused on the task at hand. It often happens as a part of the supervision of church work, but the goal is to share principles, not just their application. The end result of successful coaching is a follower who can reproduce good results without constant hands-on intervention from the pastor. When the pastor has successfully coached a number of people to do the work of the church, the next step is to have them coach others so that there is a constant influx of people qualified to serve. This is what Paul counseled Timothy to do (2 Timothy 2:2).

Jesus was an expert coach and mentor, living with his disciples, teaching and showing them how to be ministers, answering their questions, and providing guidance for their future. He left them a very focused task, that of taking the gospel to the whole world. At one point, He sent seventy disciples to practice what He had taught them and rejoiced when they returned successfully, reproducing His ministry (Luke 10).

A mentor has a slightly different relationship to a person than a coach in that he provides longer-term advice and support that is not necessarily focused on a task. The mentor is a wise counselor that helps the believer develop personally and make good decisions. Whereas a coaching relationship is focused and short term, a mentoring relationship is broader and more long term, often encompassing decades. A mentor is like a spiritual father or mother that the person can reach out to when needed, or who can intervene in the life of a person to offer guidance.

Questions

1. How convinced are you of the necessity of prayer for success in ministry? How much time do you devote to it on a weekly basis? Do you go on personal prayer retreats?

2. Do you have a defined and published curriculum to move new converts from infancy to maturity as Christians? Does this include experiences/activities as well as classes?

3. Have you received a counseling course to prepare you for pastoral counseling?

4. Have you identified leaders to coach or mentor? These will be your disciples. List their names below and what work you see them doing in the future.

Chapter 3: The Pastor as Leader

Definition of Leadership

A pastor also functions as a leader to the church. A general definition of a leader in an organization is someone that has influence on the course of the organization.[9] Leadership may be defined by position or by influence, and in a church, the pastor usually has both.

Leadership as defined here is different from management. We will be referring to some very specific activities of a leader, in contrast to those of the manager, which will be addressed in chapter 4. A major difference is that a leader has a vision of the future, while the manager is concerned about the present.

How to Get Vision

Without vision there is no direction for the pastor and his followers. No matter how good a minister he may be, the congregation that follows will not be able to mobilize its efforts in the right direction if the leader doesn't have and communicate a clear vision.

First of all, the vision must be greater than the pastor. It must originate with God and be received with great urgency and passion. It cannot be coldly crafted, given by another man, or accepted with reservations. The vision from God must be powerful enough that the pastor must commit to its accomplishment or be willing to die trying. At some point, the vision will be tested, and the pastor must have the strength to confront God with the vision commanded by Him. Without this type of vision, many begin a work for God and then turn back, despite the words of Jesus:

> *No man, having put his hand to the plough, and looking back, is fit for the kingdom of God. Luke 9:62*

Along with the vision, there is a sense of responsibility to accomplish the vision that is felt the person receiving the vision. The word *burden* has often been used to describe the sense of responsibility and sorrow if the vision is not accomplished. The Old Testament used the word *burden* to indicate some work for which a person was accountable to God:

> *And when Aaron and his sons have made an end of covering the sanctuary, and all the vessels of the sanctuary, as the camp is to set forward: after that, the sons of Kohath shall come to bear it; but they shall not touch any holy thing, lest they die. These things are <u>the burden</u> of the sons of Kohath in the tabernacle of the congregation. Numbers 4:15*

> *And this is the charge of <u>their burden</u>, according to all their service in the tabernacle of the congregation; the boards of the tabernacle, and the bars thereof, and the pillars thereof, and sockets thereof. Numbers 4:31*

Moses used the same word to refer to the responsibility of leading God's people, which was then shared with seventy elders, thus changing its meaning to a nonphysical responsibility.

> *And Moses said unto the Lord, wherefore hast thou afflicted thy servant? And wherefore have I not found favor in thy sight, that thou layest <u>the burden of all</u> these people upon me? Numbers 11:11*

> *And I will come down and talk with thee there: and I will take of the spirit which is upon thee and will put it upon them; and they shall bear <u>the burden of the people</u> with thee that thou bear it not thyself alone. Numbers 4:17*

Old Testament prophets used the word *burden* to indicate a vision of the work that God would perform upon heathen nations (Isaiah 13:1, Jeremiah 23:33, Nahum 1:1, and others). The spiritual sense of this word as it morphs through the Old Testament is that the work of the vision included a *burden* that was difficult and maybe even painful.

Paul explains his zeal for the church planting life by saying that he wants to seize (apprehend) that which had seized him—the high calling of God:

> *Not as though I had already attained, either were already perfect: but I follow after, if that I <u>may apprehend</u> that for which also I am apprehended of Christ Jesus. Philippians 3:12*

A leader with a vision from God feels a *burden* for the work of God in a particular city or to a particular group of people. It *seizes* him; it is something constant and compelling, and the leader is compelled to work out that vision regardless of personal cost. It becomes his first thought when he wakes and his last thought when he goes to sleep. It will propel him to heights of faith that he never envisioned and will fuel him through depths of defeat and frustration. Vision and burden are two key components of pastoral leadership.

A Greater Vision

While a pastor cannot make up a vision or fake a burden, he is nevertheless responsible for working out the details of the vision. At times, he may ask God for a renewal or an increase of that vision. During a time in my life when I was praying for an increase in vision, God gave me a greater vision than just a few churches, but a vision of many congregations throughout the city. My challenge since then has been how to restructure the work that we do so that people all throughout the city may have access to the gospel. My burden for the work has increased, and the requirement of greater sacrifices has been placed upon my life.

Greater vision requires more boldness. In Acts chapter 4, after the great miracle of the lame man being healed shook up the religious establishment, the church was threatened and told not to speak any further in the name of Jesus. However, fired up with a greater vision, and believing God for more signs and wonders, they prayed for boldness.

> *And when they had prayed, the place was shaken where they were assembled together; and that they were all filled with the Holy Ghost, and they spake the word of God with boldness. Acts 4:31*

Sometimes resistance and persecution will occur when a leader rises with a greater vision. We can look at the life of Nehemiah as he felt a burden and worked out the vision that God gave him, that of restoring the city of Jerusalem. It began when he...

> *... sat down and wept, and mourned certain days, and fasted, and prayed before the God of heaven.*
> Nehemiah 1:4

Although God's favor was with him as he went before the king, there was opposition from within and without (Nehemiah chapters 1-8). But Nehemiah was faithful to his vision and continued in his work of rebuilding the walls of the city. Later, he is so serious about maintaining the purity of the vision that he gets violent with some that would hinder the accomplishment of the vision.

> *And I contended with them, and cursed them, and smote certain of them, and plucked off their hair, and made them swear by God, saying, you shall not give your daughters unto their sons, nor take their daughters unto your sons, or for yourselves.*
> Nehemiah 13:25

That's someone passionate about a vision! I applaud the passion, but I would not recommend the hair-pulling technique for church leaders today (although one may be tempted!).

Pastors should be prepared to flesh out the vision given by God, and always pray for greater vision, confident that God will answer according to His riches in glory.

Vision, Mission, Strategy and Goals...

In a church, a leader is someone that can help create, define, and communicate a vision for ministry. Starting a new church, the pastor begins with a vision for winning people in a particular location, and that energizes him to work. He communicates that vision to others, and a core group begins the work of gathering souls for the kingdom of God.

Much has been written about the work of leaders. According to Kouzes and Posner,[10] great leaders get extraordinary accomplishments in organizations by five exemplary practices: they Model the Way, Inspire a Shared Vision, Challenge the Process, Enable Others to Act, and Encourage the Heart. These are all qualities that make a leader effective in getting others to buy into the common vision.

Various writers define vision and mission in different ways. Here, *vision* is defined as that overall mental picture of the future desired, while *mission* is the work necessary to get to that future. *Strategy* is the way the mission is accomplished in the here and now, and *goals* are the specific steps by which the strategy is applied to the current year.

The Vision of the Church

Jesus had a vision for a triumphant church before which the very gates of hell could not stand (Matthew 16:18). His death on the cross was motivated by a vision of the joy set before Him (Hebrews 12:2), which was nothing more than the salvation of humanity.

In his book *Developing a Vision for Ministry in the 21st Century*, Aubrey Malphurs says, "Vision is crucial to any ministry. Ministry without vision is like a surgeon without a scalpel, a cowboy who has lost his horse, a carpenter with a broken hammer."[11]

Communicating the Vision

Every leader is fueled by a personal vision of the work God has appointed for him. That vision then must be communicated to the people to motivate their work and provide direction. Moses received a vision for the Israelites of a land "flowing with milk and honey":

> *And I (God) am come down to deliver them out of the hand of the Egyptians, and to bring them up out of that land unto a good land and a large, unto a land flowing with milk and honey; unto the place of the Canaanites, and the Hittites, and the Amorites, and the Perizzites, and the Hivites, and the Jebusites. Exodus 3:8*

Moses expounded on that vision, comparing it to the land of Egypt:

> *For the land, whither thou goest in to possess it, is not as the land of Egypt, from whence ye came out, where thou sowedst thy seed, and wateredst it with thy foot, as a garden of herbs:*

> *But the land, whither ye go to possess it, is a land of hills and valleys, and drinketh water of the rain of heaven:*

> *A land which the LORD thy God careth for: the eyes of the LORD thy God are always upon it, from the beginning of the year even unto the end of the year.*
>
> *And it shall come to pass, if ye shall hearken diligently unto my commandments which I command you this day, to love the LORD your God, and to serve him with all your heart and with all your soul,*
>
> *That I will give you the rain of your land in his due season, the first rain and the latter rain, that thou mayest gather in thy corn, and thy wine, and thine oil.*
>
> *And I will send grass in thy fields for thy cattle, that thou mayest eat and be full. Deuteronomy 11:10-15*

This vision fired up the people to leave Egypt behind and travel across the desert to the new land. Unfortunately, a majority without vision (unbelief) lost their way in the desert, and the nation could not enter into the promised land until forty years later.

Paul in the New Testament is sent out with a vision of taking the gospel throughout the region and finds that the Holy Spirit changes the vision as they travel. For example, although he began trying to reach Jews, he got more of a response from the Gentiles:

> *Then Paul and Barnabas waxed bold, and said, It was necessary that the word of God should first have been spoken to you: but seeing ye put it from you, and judge yourselves unworthy of everlasting life, lo, we turn to the Gentiles.*

> *For so hath the Lord commanded us, saying, I have set thee to be a light of the Gentiles, that thou shouldest be for salvation unto the ends of the earth.*
>
> *And when the Gentiles heard this, they were glad, and glorified the word of the Lord: and as many as were ordained to eternal life believed. Acts 13:46-48*

He continues traveling and is forbidden from preaching in some regions, but is directed to Macedonia, where he pioneers the Philippian church and others.

> *Now when they had gone throughout Phrygia and the region of Galatia, and were forbidden of the Holy Ghost to preach the word in Asia,*
>
> *After they were come to Mysia, they assayed to go into Bithynia: but the Spirit suffered them not.*
>
> *And they passing by Mysia came down to Troas.*
>
> *And a vision appeared to Paul in the night; There stood a man of Macedonia, and prayed him, saying, Come over into Macedonia, and help us.*
>
> *And after he had seen the vision, immediately we endeavoured to go into Macedonia, assuredly gathering that the Lord had called us for to preach the gospel unto them. Acts 16:6-10*

The mission is the particular way that a vision will be accomplished. All Christians are called to go preach throughout the whole world, but the mission specifically may encompass only a part of that world—a city, a state, a country, or a people. The mission is the way that we accomplish the vision that Jesus left of a glorious church. In order to accomplish that, God gives us a personal vision of a church in a location, or a type of people that we will reach as we move forward in our mission.

As time passes, the vision and mission may become more defined and specific. Perhaps the church has a unique ministry that will be emphasized, or it is called to a unique ethnic or language group. This calls for the pastor and the leadership team to craft a *vision statement* for the church that is simple and powerful. Along with vision, there needs to be a mission statement, as well as strategy and goals that will move the church forward into the vision.

The vision statement of the church should be written down and be visible and available to all. It should include the ministry's purpose and mission, its values and strategy, and the people and location to be served. The crafting of this vision statement should involve the leadership of the church so that they will buy into it and be willing to own it and express it. For a sample of a vision statement, see appendix I.

In a small church, people are motivated to work by their relationship with the pastor. As the church grows larger, the pastor is no longer able to have a close relationship with everyone, so the motivation has to change from a person (pastor) to a vision. Thus, the preparation and communication of the vision has to become an integral part of the leadership communication. The pastor has to grow intentionally as a leader and present the vision to other leaders in the church and to the congregation on a regular basis.

The Mission of the Church

After vision has been established, the mission and strategy of the church can be defined.

Mission is what the ministry is supposed to be doing to accomplish the vision. Vision is descriptive and may be lengthy, but mission should be concise and powerful. A church may conceive of a vision first, and then develop a mission, or the process may happen in reverse order.

While vision moves the heart, the mission is more intellectual. It answers the questions of whom do we want to reach and how exactly will we do that in the context of the community. Even more than vision, mission needs to be stated and published. It should be memorable enough that every leader can remember it by heart, and it should be visible and prominent in the church facilities. A *mission statement* prepares the ground for its strategy and goals.

Values that derive from the vision and mission help the leadership decide what is important. Is it more important to be in the worship service or to be preparing the lunch to be served afterwards? Is it more important to be on time for church or to be late if picking up a visitor to Sunday service? A thousand such choices face every believer and congregation, and the leadership through their words and example set the values that will move the congregation in its mission.

Sample Mission Statement

- The mission of Northwood Community Church is to be used of God in helping people become fully functioning followers of Christ.[12]

Strategy

The strategy of the local church may change from time to time as goals are accomplished or the mission is modified. This change has to be intentional and based on evaluations of past strategies that either worked or did not. When establishing a new strategy, it is important to make sure that the leadership is on board before making an announcement to all. Goals and timetables have to be defined with the leadership before letting the congregation know that they will be teaching Bible studies, doing outreach on Saturdays, or having special evangelistic events.

The strategy defined must then direct all the events and activities of the church, so that the body is in one accord. Any activity or event that is not part of the strategy has to be eliminated! This may include "historical" structures, favorite programs, and any new efforts to achieve a goal.

In *Simple Church*, Thom Rainer and Eric Geiger discuss the power of doing away with church busyness to focus on God's business of saving souls. "To have a simple church, you must design a simple discipleship process. This process must be clear. It must move people into maturity. It must be integrated fully into your church, and you must get rid of the clutter around it."[13] In their investigations, they found that simple churches statistically exhibited more growth and vitality than other churches. More on this in a later chapter.

Unfortunately, many churches engage in activities just to keep people busy. Committee meetings, youth events, choir rehearsals, and social outings take the place of effective evangelism and discipleship. The leadership may not stop to ask how this activity either develops believers or brings in new converts. But at some point, this hard question needs to be asked and the branches pruned for greater growth.

Strategy is used to establish goals that will move the church forward. Each goal is a specific milestone that moves the strategy forward. Goals have to be carefully defined and articulated and are best focused on activities that are clearly under the control of the church and not dependent on outside circumstances or people.

Defining Good Goals

Michael Hyatt, *NY Times* best-selling author and coach to CEOs of major companies, defines SMARTER goals.[14] Following are some definitions of SMARTER goals in the context of church work:

SMARTER Goals are:

> *Specific*: the actual activity is focused and detailed.
> *Measurable*: the goal is related to some number or date for its completion.
> *Actionable*: the goal is something active that can be seen and clearly defined.
> *Risky*: good goals are beyond the comfort zone and cause the church to stretch and grow in order to achieve them.
> *Time-keyed*: every goal needs to be aligned with a time frame. Achievement goals should have a deadline; habit goals should have a frequency.
> *Exciting*: goals should be related to important values of the church so that work is meaningful, not boring.
> *Relevant*: goals must be appropriate to the overall philosophy and vision of the church.

For example, a worthwhile goal would be a certain number of weekly Bible studies taught, flyers passed out, or people invited to church. Although sometimes things like attendance or numbers of baptisms are given as goals, those would better be defined as the results of our goals, since those outcomes are dependent on God adding to the church (Acts 2:47).

Finally, goals cannot be just ideas that are shared in a leadership meeting or retreat. They should be written down carefully and shared with all those involved, and when appropriate, the whole church. Staff, volunteers, and church members should be recruited into the work to achieve the goals. Progress towards the goals should be evaluated a few times in the year (quarterly or semiannually). Scheduled evaluations also allow the possibility of modifying or completely scrapping the goals if the circumstances require it.

Questions

1. Do you have a written vision statement for your church that you can remember and your leaders know by heart? If not, can you set a goal to craft one by a specific date?

2. What are some values for your church that drive and represent your vision?

3. Have you defined a strategy and goals for how you will work in the near term to fulfill the Great Commission?

4. What specific steps can you take in the next six months to grow your leadership ability in the four areas: vision, mission, strategy, and goals?

Chapter 4: The Pastor as Manager

Note: in everyday language, many people use the words *management* and *leadership* in confusing ways. To make things consistent here, I have defined both terms in very specific ways defined by the activities that are done and not the personal qualities of the doer. I understand that a person may use the personal quality of leadership when managing others, but if the focus is on the *work*, then the activity falls under management in this context.

Definition of Church Work

Pastors have the job of organizing the church for work. Work can be evangelizing, running a service, or taking care of a building. The process is still the same: *defining the tasks to be done, motivating people to do it, setting up the structure that will be used, assigning people to various roles, and supervising the work.* The tendency for pastors is to simply copy the structure that is traditional in their experience, find someone to put in charge, and hope it all works out. Unfortunately, this type of haphazard approach to church structure can hinder growth and can cause a variety of problems.

The Bible uses two metaphors for understanding the functioning of the church: it is a *body* and it is a *building*. In today's words, we could say the church is both an *organism* and an *organization*. In various places of the New Testament, the apostles mix metaphors to coin such interesting concepts as the "edifying of the body" and "growing of a temple" made of "lively stones."

> Ye also, as <u>lively stones</u>, are built up a spiritual house, an holy priesthood, to offer up spiritual sacrifices, acceptable to God by Jesus Christ. 1 Peter 2:5
>
> And are built upon the foundation of the apostles and prophets, Jesus Christ himself being the chief corner stone; Ephesians 2:20
>
> In whom all the building fitly framed together <u>groweth unto an holy temple</u> in the Lord: Ephesians 2:21
>
> In whom ye also are builded together for an habitation of God through the Spirit. Ephesians 2:22
>
> For the perfecting of the saints, for the work of the ministry, for the <u>edifying of the body</u> of Christ: Ephesians 4:12
>
> For we are labourers together with God: ye are God's <u>husbandry</u>, ye are God's <u>building</u>. 1 Corinthians 3:9

How to Get Wisdom

The most important quality to have when a pastor begins to organize the church is *wisdom*. It requires a great deal of wisdom to put together teams and select leaders. It requires

Chapter 4: The Pastor as Manager

wisdom to know what work to do exactly when, how to communicate goals and priorities to others, how to encourage and train workers, how to supervise the work, and how and when to give praise.

Wisdom and knowledge are two different things. Knowledge is information, but wisdom is the ability to use that information correctly to get to the desired goal. Today's world offers an excess of knowledge through every possible media. It is possible to have a great deal of knowledge and very little wisdom. In fact, too much knowledge can be confusing and misleading if we do not know how to apply it to the situation at hand.

Solomon felt the need for wisdom as he considered how great a work it was to lead the people of God. He asked God for wisdom and knowledge:

> *Give me now wisdom and knowledge, that I may go out and come in before this people: for who can judge this thy people, that is so great?*
> *2 Chronicles 1:10*

God honored his request, giving him more wisdom than *all the children of the East country, and all the wisdom of Egypt* (1 Kings 4:30). Solomon showed great wisdom in his judgment of the two women and the dead child (1 Kings 3:16-28), and he expounded the importance of it all throughout the books of Proverbs and Ecclesiastes. In one instance, he said *wisdom is the principal thing* (Proverbs 1:7). Solomon emphasized the importance of wisdom by saying, among other things, that God created the world using wisdom (Proverbs 3:19), and that wisdom is needed to build a home (Proverbs 24:3).

Given the importance of wisdom to manage the church, how do we get more? The only way is simply to ask God:

> *If any of you <u>lack wisdom</u>, let him ask of God, that giveth to all men liberally, and upbraideth not: and it shall be given him. But let him ask in faith, nothing wavering. James 1:5-6a*

Sometimes we use our human wisdom to do the work of managing the church. The result may be confusion and disagreement. It is easy to make mistakes when dealing with complex situations while lacking all the facts. But when we operate in the wisdom that is from God, the result is positive and peaceful. James contrasts the two types of wisdom:

> *But if you have bitter envying and strife in your hearts, glory not, and lie not against the truth. This wisdom descendeth not from above, but is earthly, sensual, devilish.*
>
> *For where envying and strife is, there is confusion and every evil work.*
>
> *But the <u>wisdom that is from above</u> is first pure, then peaceable, gentle, and easy to be entreated, full of mercy and good fruits, without partiality, and without hypocrisy. James 3:14-17*

Pastors should pray for wisdom every day, confident that God will answer according to His riches in glory.

The Structure of the Church

Most structure elements of a church (departments, ministries, etc.) are typically organized either as *affinity groups* or as *work groups*. An *affinity group* is one composed of people that share a particular characteristic, such as age (youth group), status (single mothers), or interest (fishing). The benefit of an affinity group is the identification of the needs of a homogeneous group, which can then be met through the group's association. A drawback to such groups is that they may not have a clear focus and goal, and may become, in time, just a social gathering.

Still, affinity events are very useful to develop people in the church and bring in new converts. One example of a very useful affinity event is a couples' seminar that can bring in new believers while also ministering to church members.

While social interactions are needed in the church, there are worthwhile goals to pursue while allowing the group naturally to fulfill the social needs. Considering that, *work groups* may be more useful than affinity groups, although the latter are traditional in many churches.

Work groups (teams) are those that bring people together for a time with a clear goal in mind. For example, the music team is a work group where people come together to accomplish the goal of providing anointed music for church services. There is a sense of team and mission that gathers around that type of group, and the success of the group can be easily measured, as well as the contribution of each member. Other teams that a church may have, for example, are an evangelism team, the usher/welcome team, and a Sunday school team. One aspect of such teams is that they exist to fulfill a need. If the need changes or no longer exists, teams can be phased out in a positive manner as having achieved their goal.

The Wisdom of Teams

Teams are groups of people organized to accomplish a goal. It is more effective to form teams to do church jobs than to assign a single person to do it. The benefits of creating teams to accomplish tasks/goals are many.

According to Katzenbach and Smith,[15] teams are more effective because they create:

- Commitment to a common vision,
- Synergy from complementary talents,
- Greater focus to accomplish a task, and
- Future leaders through hands-on training.

George Cladis writes about the effective use of teams for church work in today's postmodern world: "The most effective churches today are the ones that are developing team-based leadership. This pattern will likely continue into the twenty-first century, both because Scripture emphasizes Spirit-led, Spirit-gifted, collaborative teams fellowship and because today's culture is receptive to such leadership."[16]

In order to function well, teams require good *systems* to accomplish the work. Systems are processes that are repeated in a cyclical way. Good systems help assure continuity and improvements over time. Church systems make the functioning of the body of Christ more effective and easier to maintain.

A team approach to building church structure also works well in start-up churches in that teams may be formed as needs are identified. A new church just starting may not need many departments and ministries, while a more complex structure may suit a larger church. A few teams with just two or three people each are probably enough to handle the needs of a small congregation.

However, from the start, each team needs to have a clear mission, goals, structure, and measurable outcomes, and the leader should be informed that their job as leader is temporary with a fixed duration (six months or a year). That way, when team leaders are changed, the pastor may avoid hurting the feelings of people being moved out of a leadership position.

A pastor needs wisdom to set up the structure of the church intentionally. That is, the needs of the church must be considered, an appropriate structure must be set up, and the right people must be placed on the teams. Rather than appointing a leader right away, I have had success being the leader of a newly formed team and observing which member rises to the level of leadership through their desire and ability. Then, I withdraw from the team while appointing the natural leader who is likely to be accepted by the rest of the team due to his or her performance.

Wisdom comes from God and is known by the response of people, as we read in James 3:17. This is the kind of wisdom needed to prepare a good team structure for the church.

Home Fellowship Groups

Home fellowship groups (cell groups) have been used by many churches successfully for a variety of purposes.[17] They have been used with a Bible study format, with an evangelism format, with a fellowship format, or some combination of these three. There are churches that have such cell groups as part of the ministry tools, while other churches are based on the cell group concept as a cornerstone. These are two radically different concepts.

Having meetings in the houses of believers is a biblical concept, as found in Acts 2:46-47 and various other places in the New Testament. However, the Bible does not say exactly what went on in such meetings. Were they focused on evangelism or prayer? Did they have worship? How long was the sharing of the Word, etc.? This leaves the actual format open to our interpretation or decision.

Such meetings, if structured and well supervised, supplement the regular services of the church and can be a place for evangelism, fellowship, Bible study, and even development of leaders. A deliberate decision needs to be made by the pastor as to the purpose of the house meetings in the local church, and then the format carefully planned to fit the purpose.

The most important benefit of cell groups of any format is that they provide a way for new Christians to quickly connect with other believers, which will help them to become assimilated into the church. This is an effective technique to close the back door to the church, so that new Christians are retained.

There are many resources for learning how to set up cell groups in the church. There are some excellent books by Christian authors and many large churches have used the cell group format successfully.

Management Skills

Most pastors do not begin their ministry thinking that they will need managerial skills to be successful. However, the growth of the church probably rests on this aspect of the work more than any other. The pastor needs to develop skills to identify needs, create teams, motivate people, place them in the right area to work, and supervise them appropriately. The pastor has to develop personally in areas like organizational leadership, communication, corporate finances, time management, and supervisory principles.

This can be done through a personal plan of development. The first challenge is understanding that the growth of the church does depend on the pastor's success in organizing the church to work. Then the pastor must gain the appropriate knowledge through classes and seminars or a formal course of study to develop management skills.

Situational Leadership (a management technique)

Most people naturally manage others in the way they prefer to be managed. The thinking is that since I like to be supervised in this manner, I will treat others in the way I want to be treated. While this is a good biblical principle for personal relationships (the Golden Rule), management relationships are more complicated.

Managers need to lead other people in the best way for *followers to be successful*. Surprisingly, the followers' way may not be the leader's way. For example, I may prefer to be given a task and then be left alone to meet all the challenges and conquer them. If my supervisor frequently asks me how I am doing and if I need help, I would find that kind of attention unsettling. However, someone else may prefer to be given a task and for the supervisor to continue providing guidance and support along the way. Failure to do that may be seen as a lack of interest in the task or in the person. Clearly these are different ways to work.

"Situational Leadership," as developed by Ken Blanchard,[18] is a management approach as defined here. It is based on the fact that in any management situation there is a focus on *the task* and a focus on *the relationship*. Some managers focus more on the task, while others may focus more on the relationship. A task-focused approach (*Directive*) can achieve more, but at the risk of affecting relationships. A relationship-focused approach (*Supportive*) nourishes the relationships but may not accomplish the goal.

Based on these two parameters, the management relationship can be structured in one of four styles: Directing, Coaching, Supporting, and Delegating.

- Directing Manager: relationship is *high* on giving direction and *low* on support.
- Coaching Manager: relationship is *high* on direction and *high* on support.
- Supporting Manager: relationship is *low* on direction and *high* on support.
- Delegating Manager: relationship is *low* on direction and support.

The manager has to assess the motivation and ability of the employee/volunteer to determine which leadership style will be most successful. Then the manager has to act in the appropriate style. While this simple analysis can help point the way, the real work of the leader is to learn to work in all four leadership styles so that he can have success with different kinds of people.

Personality and Spiritual Gifts

One way to grow personally and to develop leaders in the church is to use a personality inventory or a spiritual gift inventory. These are surveys that help people figure out their preferred mode of thinking and behaving (personality). There are no right or wrong personalities or gifts, these tools simply help people see where they might best fit in the structure of the church. These are useful also for the pastor as he evaluates himself and his staff and seeks to place people in the right places.

A number of these surveys are listed as "spiritual gifts surveys," and they apply to various Christian giftedness, ministry positions, and manifestations of the Holy Spirit. Most come in some version that includes the items found in Romans 12:3-8, 1 Corinthians 12, and 1 Peter 4:9-11. Many of them can be found online via a search. They should be used with wisdom according to the needs of the local church.

Personality inventories like the Briggs-Meyers,[19] temperament analysis, and other personality tests give insight into the preferred mode of behavior of people in organizations. This knowledge is important for pastoral staff and teams as the church desires to move forward in quality and numbers. We will look more closely at these tools in a later chapter.

Church Health and Systems

Various Christian writers have studied the factors across cultural and denominational lines that promote church health and church growth. The underlying assumption is that, just as a healthy body is a growing body, a healthy church will grow in numbers. So rather than trying to achieve numerical growth by any means, the emphasis is on establishing the right structure or systems that will result in a healthy church.

As mentioned earlier, the Bible refers to the church as a body and also as a building. The body metaphor is important in that it leads to a study of the church as an organism with different organs (members). The building metaphor is important because it leads to a study of the structure of the church (organization). These views are complementary, and in nature we see a close relationship between structure and function. Thus, in the church, as well as in the human body, good systems lead to health.

All churches use systems, cyclical patterns of behavior that accomplish a desired goal. Once a system is created, it impacts behavior in such a way that any new parts of the system will conform to the established way of doing things. Even families function based on systems, and Family Systems Therapy has been used for many years to help change the dysfunctional behavior of groups and individuals. Just as in physiology and in families, the health of the church is the result of all the systems working together.

We will look at more information on church structure and church systems in chapter 9.

Management of Finances

Finances is one area of management that can be a great blessing or a great hindrance to the development of the local church. Recently, several pastors personally known to me have been severely affected by financial problems, and some have left the pastorate due to them. There is not enough space in this short book to discuss all the principles of sound finances. A few paragraphs will serve to address this topic, while referring the reader to other resources for further study.[20]

There are many references in the Old Testament to funds being provided by people for a godly purpose. Early in the wilderness, the people gave sacrificially for the preparation of the tabernacle. Their generosity was so outstanding that Moses had to tell them to stop giving (Exodus 36:1-7). Later the temple became the place where people brought their tithes and offerings, and Malachi writes that God considers this practice a commandment to be obeyed (Malachi 3:8-11).

In the New Testament, we see that the early church also put together resources to meet the needs of the local congregation. We find the beginning of this practice in Acts 4, when people sell their properties and bring the proceeds to the leadership. The immediate need that is referenced in Acts, chapter 6, is the feeding of destitute widows. There are further references to financial matters and provision for the needy in Acts, chapters 5 and 6.

Chapter 4: The Pastor as Manager

> *Neither was there any among them that lacked: for as many as were possessors of lands or houses sold them, and brought the prices of the things that were sold, And laid them down at the apostles' feet: and distribution was made unto every man according as he had need. And Joses, who by the apostles was surnamed Barnabas, (which is, being interpreted, The son of consolation,) a Levite, and of the country of Cyprus, Having land, sold it, and brought the money, and laid it at the apostles' feet.*
> Acts 4:34-37

Finally, there are various references in the epistles about the apostle Paul taking up an offering to send to the poor saints in Jerusalem (2 Corinthians 8-9).

We can conclude from these Scriptures that it is a godly principle for believers to pool their assets to help one another, and to provide for resources that are consecrated to God's use. So how do we do it best today in our time and place?

Principles

To begin, there are three principles that every pastor should keep in mind:

1. Pastors are accountable to God. The church's money is God's money. Whether we refer to tithing, offerings, or special fundraising funds, once funds are designated for a spiritual purpose, they become the property of God on earth. Thus, the pastors are stewards of what belongs to Him and must demonstrate respect and wisdom in using it for His purposes—as He would have it, not as we would have it. A clear conscience before God in this aspect will prepare the way for the other two principles below.

2. Pastors are accountable to the people. As managers of the funds deposited with the church, pastors are responsible to protect, administer, and invest according to the interests and wishes of the people that contributed. As pastors, we have a great deal of latitude in how we use funds, and that should create in us a great desire to do this job the very best way possible. Many times, there is a church board to whom we report financial matters. All things should be done with integrity and honesty, especially when mistakes are made. Having a yearly budget and following it will help the financial administration and reporting at all levels.[21]

3. Pastors are accountable to government agencies. Operating as a nonprofit organization in the United States brings many benefits, including relief from sales tax, freedom from having to report financial matters yearly (as other nonprofits are required to do), and the ability to access various donors, including local and federal government sources.

But with those benefits also come some responsibilities, which include being accountable to officials or agencies at times. If we manage finances well according to the first two principles above, that will go a long way toward satisfying this third principle. But there are laws and regulations that guide the use of finances, and these are not difficult to meet with a little attention and work.[22] However, even if we are meeting the requirement of a good conscience toward God and the people, we may be in violation of state or federal regulations in our handling of money. Today's pastor cannot remain uninformed but must seek good counsel in this area through a local CPA or other church financial expert.

Major Financial Concerns

The two major sources of financial stress for most churches today are paying a mortgage or rent on a building and paying the salary of the pastor and other staff.

Having an adequate building for meeting on Sundays is a necessity due to the way our churches are organized today. But if we focus more on reaching people in their homes, a building becomes less important, and this can alleviate some of the stress from having and maintaining a building.

If a building is needed, the correct perspective is to have one *proportionate* to the finances and lifestyle of the congregation. This may be difficult to do if the pastor has a different financial status or lifestyle than the people in the congregation. In such a case, the pastor has to adjust to the people he leads, and not vice versa.

The same principle of *proportion* applies to salaries paid to employees of the church, including the pastor. Salaries should be appropriate to the finances and lifestyle of the congregation, so that the paid staff are not living below or beyond the means of the people in the church. This may require that the pastor adjust his living expenses accordingly, or that he or his family secure other employment to achieve a higher personal income if desired.

We see that the early church put their resources together and gathered funds to help the needy, not to purchase property or to pay Apostolic salaries! If financial commitments to a building and salaries do not allow the church to help those in need, we are not following the Apostolic pattern of church finances, and our priorities should be revised. Clearly, making a change midstream is not easy, but thinking about finances the right way should help us to refocus and make room for the ministry of helping the poor.

Balance between Faith and Facts

The most difficult balancing act in the area of finances is that between operating in *faith* (God will provide if I take a step of faith) and *facts* (how much money is in the bank today). I have seen good pastors in similar situations get different results: one takes a leap of faith successfully and the other one leaps as well but falls! Looking from the outside, I cannot see a difference between one and the other—is there hidden lack of integrity or sin that caused one to fail? I really can't judge. All I can do is to search my heart and take steps of faith, while at the same time moving slowly enough to see some results of my faith in action before I leap.

Every pastor needs to understand this balance and move forward considering both points of views. There are times that God will provide miraculously, and there are other times that God will ask us to work. I have seen both in my personal experience as a pastor.

Recently we outgrew the facility where we meet, and after considering various choices, I took the stand before Him, in fear and trembling, that I wanted direction from above. As I began to pray, I felt that the Lord was guiding me in a new direction. I prayed for confirmation from Him, and it came by way of our building owner, who called me and granted us the last two years of our mortgage as a corporate gift! This was almost forty thousand dollars (a large quantity to me)—what a miracle! But after that, God has left it in our hands to take the next financial step, much in the same manner as He had done in previous years.

How can we understand all this? Well, God is able to do financial miracles, but He also wants us, as a body, to work and provide the resources needed. How do we know which one we are to do? There are no rules; it's a living relationship with our

Father, and He will let us know in His time what we should do today. The proof is in the results.

Fundraising

Fundraising as a special activity has been controversial for some pastors. It can be suspect if we are simply copying the corporate America way of doing things. The key issue is what are we fundraising for? Earlier, we referred to the Apostolic pattern for the use of funds, but most pastors today engage in special fundraising to help pay for building expenses as the most demanding financial effort of a church. Each one should operate according to a clear conscience before God.

Besides considering the purpose of the money being raised, our attitude toward raising funds also should be examined. Henri Nouwen in *The Spirituality of Fundraising*, says, "Fundraising is proclaiming what we believe in such a way that we offer other people opportunities to participate with us in our vision and mission. Fundraising is precisely the opposite of begging."[23] With that perspective in mind, the pastor should be confident that any funds given for a godly purpose mean more than the same amounts used for personal earthly purposes. The only caveat in that last statement is that the pastor should encourage giving, but never use pressure or guilt feelings, allowing people to set the right priorities in their own lives.

A very accessible parachurch group (The Rocket Company) has developed a practical seminar on church fundraising,[24] including helpful discussions on the five reasons people give, the five seasons of giving, and the five systems to increase giving.

One of the most practical takeaways from this seminar is an understanding of the five different types of givers and how to connect with all of them. According to the authors, people give in response to *need*, in response to *vision*, in response to *education* about giving, out of *obedience,* and due to a *relationship* to the pastor. When preparing a special fundraiser, or even in weekly collections, the pastor and staff should be mindful to cover all five reasons for giving in order to motivate all givers in the congregation.

This seminar and ancillary materials prepares the pastor to connect with all types of givers and to plan a yearlong calendar of activities to enhance giving as a Christian discipline.

Get Help Early!

The final point in this short treatment is that pastors should reach out and get sound financial advice before it's too late! Sometimes fear or embarrassment causes pastors to avoid taking this step, and the issue becomes a larger problem either in the credibility of the pastor or with a government agency.

There is a lot of help available for pastors in this area of the business of a church. The brevity of the treatment in this book is not a reflection of its importance, but a recognition that there are many excellent resources that can help.

Questions

1. What kind of structural model are you using for your church? How effective is it in achieving your goals?

2. Have you set up teams to do the work of the church? If not, how will you go about implementing teams for greater success?

3. What is your preferred mode of managing (leading style)? Directing, Coaching, Supporting, or Delegating?

How is it impacting your relationship with your church staff/volunteers?

4. Can you identify the parts of some church systems in your congregation? Which one might require the most improvement right now, and what will you do in the next three months to improve it?

5. How would you rate your financial management of church funds (scale of 1–5, where 5 is excellent and 1 is poor)?

   1   2   3   4   5

6. What step will you take this month to improve the financial outlook of your church?

PART 2: FURTHER APPLICATIONS

This section of the book presents some specific applications of the job of the pastor in areas important for growth.

Caution!

In the next chapters, there is a lot of information presented in a condensed format. The purpose of these chapters is to introduce various important topics, not present them in an exhaustive manner. However, you can use the references cited to explore each topic in greater depth according to your need or interest.

In the Area of Ministry

>   Chapter 5: Assimilation, Discipleship, and Retention
>   Chapter 6: Discipleship and Church Growth

In the Area of Leadership

>   Chapter 7: Focus on the Leader
>   Chapter 8: More on Leadership

In the Area of Management

Chapter 9: Church Structure and Church Systems
Chapter 10: Key Performance Indicators for Measuring
              Church Health

You will find the Endnotes section at the end of the book.

MINISTRY

Chapter 5: Assimilation, Discipleship, and Retention

A Love for Souls

Busy with grasping much information about the work of the pastor, some of it very technical, it is possible to lose track of the most important qualification of a minister—*a love for souls.*

As pastors we will always be called to minister, whether to a congregation or a group of leaders, and we can never lose sight that our job is to care for their souls. A genuine *love for souls* must be the motivating factor in all the work that we do. It cannot be success, personal satisfaction, church numbers, or the admiration of other pastors and ministers.

By *soul* I mean, in the simplest of terms, the inner life of every human being. We have to learn to look beyond the bodies and the faces to the secret life inside. Everyone has a soul, and in its deepest part, it is tender, fragile, and easily hurt. If a minister cannot understand this secret about souls, it is easy to be frustrated with people. Souls come in big bodies, small bodies, male or female bodies, ugly bodies, or beautiful bodies. It doesn't make any difference; we need to look deeper to see the soul there.

Some years ago, when I was working as a counselor in a youth detention center, I had to meet with a young man that everyone feared. He had been involved in numerous crimes, including murder, and was known to be violent. I was asked if I wanted a guard outside the door as I met with this young man, but I refused. I simply silently prayed for God to give me a love for his soul.

When he came into the room, his demeanor was hard and angry, but when I began to talk to him with love in my heart, it all began to change. In just a few minutes, there were tears pouring down his face as I led him in a word of prayer for the salvation of his soul. This young man had attended church as a child, but his life had taken a wrong turn somewhere. He was hungry for God and just needed someone to demonstrate the love and mercy of our Savior. I never saw him again, but I know that both he and I left that counseling session with renewed hope in Jesus.

We cannot judge people for what they look like on the outside or even the achievements or trappings of success they may bring. Whether they have a lot of money or are very poor, the value of their soul is the same before God. James writes clearly against judging people based on their appearance in the second chapter of his epistle. He exhorts us to not discriminate in our treatment of one person versus another, calling those who do so "judges of evil thoughts" (James 2:1-15).

In the New Testament, we are often called upon to love one another and serve one another.

> And <u>walk in love</u>, as Christ also has loved us, and has given himself for us an offering and the sacrifice to God for a sweet smelling savor. Ephesians 5:2

> For brethren, you have been called unto liberty; only use not liberty for an occasion to the flesh, but <u>by love serve</u> one another. Galatians 5:13

Chapter 5: Assimilation, Discipleship, and Retention

> *My little children, let us <u>not love in word</u>, neither in tongue; but in deed and in truth. 1 John 3:18*

We must pay attention to the condition of souls when they come to Christ: they are hurt, broken, and desperate for healing. On the outside, they may be smiling, or they may be angry. Those are just defenses to protect that secret, sensitive soul. If they receive the balm of the Holy Spirit and real love, then they can begin to heal and eventually demonstrate changes in their thinking and behavior.

As ministers we have been given charge of a garden of souls. How are the souls that God has given to you? Are they healthy and growing, or are they still dead or drying? If we take good care of the souls we have now, God will give us more, but if we neglect our own garden, God will hold us accountable and withhold greater things.

The key is to realize that every soul has a need and a potential. Each one has a need that can be met by the Holy Spirit, and each one has a potential that can be realized by His Word. The church is a place where every soul can bloom in the light of God's grace to its full potential.

The Power of Assimilation

As I read about the life of the early church in Acts, chapter 2, I am often struck by the sense of community that existed. The chapter refers to their being together daily in various settings: prayer, fellowship, sharing things with one another, eating joyfully together. These things can be gathered into the term *assimilation*.

Assimilation is the sense that people have of belonging to a certain group.[25] If a church is mostly focused on having services once or twice a week, people will find it difficult to become part of the group. On the other hand, if it is easy for them to join the church group, it will become much easier to find Jesus and accept the gospel of salvation.

Part of the job of a minister is to create opportunities for people to assimilate into the church. This can come through various types of informal gatherings, personal visits, shared meals, and also more formal activities of the church.

Assimilation is a prerequisite to discipleship. People will not allow themselves to be discipled unless they feel that they are part of the church. The quality that will allow people to assimilate and be discipled is simply the love they feel from the ministers and other church members.

Some researchers estimate that only about 10% of first-time guests will remain in the church. I have confirmed similar numbers by polling a few local churches and my own church. While this is a very small number, it is a real number, and it should cause some concern. All churches will grow in numbers just by paying attention to assimilation.

In order to have good assimilation, it is important to look at each step of what happens when someone comes to church for the first time, *from their point of view.*

From Guest to Disciple

First-time guests may be apprehensive or resistant, and they are not always open to the church when they get there. Maybe they were pressured by someone to come, or they felt that they needed to come, but it was a big investment on their part to get up on a Sunday morning. So here they are, the whole family all dressed up, at a new place where they hardly know anyone, and they don't know exactly what is going to happen.

The first contact that occurs in the parking lot or the front door will set the stage for their experience. Guests need to be greeted, directed, treated kindly, and seated smoothly. Part of the greeting should be filling out a contact card to stay in touch and send more information about the church. A smile and genuine love will go a long way toward breaking the ice.

Most guests will come for the first time on a Sunday morning. Every aspect of the service should be organized with excellence for ministry to be effective. The songs must have words that can be understood by the guests (no Christianese, please), the announcements must be brief and to the point, and the message must be delivered with the guests in mind. That means inspired, short, and to the point.

Paul cautions believers to pursue love (charity), but to focus on preaching (prophesy) words of comfort, edification and exhortation, doctrine, or revelation (1 Corinthians 14:1-3 and 6). While not forbidding speaking in other tongues, he emphasizes the power of preaching to touch the heart of the visitor during a church meeting.

> *Yet in the church I had rather speak <u>five words with my understanding</u>, that by my voice I might teach others also, than ten thousand words in an unknown tongue. 1 Corinthians 14:19*

> *But if <u>all prophesy</u>, and there come in one that believeth not, or one unlearned, he is convinced of all, he is judged of all: And thus are the secrets of his heart made manifest; and so falling down on his face he will worship God, and report that God is in you of a truth. 1 Corinthians 14:24-25*

The most powerful thing that can occur in this visit, either during the service or an altar call, is for the visitor to experience the presence of God. This can happen in many ways including the manifestation of the gifts of the Spirit as outlined in Paul's first letter to the Corinthians:

> *But the manifestation of the Spirit is given to every man to profit withal.*
>
> *For to one is given by the Spirit the word of wisdom; to another the word of knowledge by the same Spirit;*
>
> *To another faith by the same Spirit; to another the gifts of healing by the same Spirit; To another the working of miracles; to another prophecy; to another discerning of spirits; to another divers kinds of tongues; to another the interpretation of tongues:*
>
> *But all these worketh that one and the selfsame Spirit, dividing to every man severally as he will.*
> *1 Corinthians 12:7-11*

After the service, a short meeting with the pastor and other leaders serves to provide a point of contact. This meeting should take place in a special area designated with visitors in mind. Here guests will converse briefly, share drinks and a simple snack, and will receive a gift bag. Finally, the guests will be informed about further contact from the follow-up team.

The response team can follow up via email or text, as well as a personal visit if so desired. A knowledge of the community will help the church find the right balance between a caring contact and intrusiveness, which may be rejected in these days of high privacy.

As the team follows up, the new guest should be apprised of three types of activities in which to participate: fun events, small groups meetings, and service through teams. Depending on the structure of the church, these can be more formal or informal, but they will be effective in helping the guest to connect with the church in some manner.

Assimilation may not seem spiritual enough to some, but I have found that if guests keep coming back to services and connect with a group, they will be saved and they will grow up in Christ.

The Growth of the Disciple

How can we disciple believers? The first thing to communicate to all is that a Christian should be learning and growing throughout their whole life. Ephesians 4:11-15 contains what has been called the five-fold ministry, which refers to offices that God has established in the church. These ministries work for the "perfecting of the saints" and set a standard for growth of the Christian. That standard, as shown in verse 13, is the "fullness of Christ." Verse 15 reaffirms this idea by saying that we should grow up into Christ.

> *Till we all come in the unity of the faith, and that of the knowledge of the son of God, unto a perfect man, unto the measure of the stature of the <u>fullness of Christ</u>. Ephesians 4:13*

The conclusion is that every Christian should continue to grow until they reach the character and maturity of Christ. I would suggest that this "fullness of Christ" will never quite be achieved by any human being this side of heaven. The challenge then is to keep growing.

The goal of discipleship is to make a lifelong investment in someone (or a few *someones*). Craig Etheredge of Discipleship.org writes that it is important to go about discipleship in the right way.[26] To be successful, one has to know how to identify disciples, choose disciples wisely, and multiply disciples. The key principle is to realize that the teacher is making a lifelong investment in a few people, the same way that Jesus taught by example.

Every new convert must realize that he/she is an infant spiritually but is responsible for continued growth as a Christian. We can study this growth in different phases, as we can do with a child that is growing up. Growing from one phase to another requires meeting some challenges and achieving maturity in some key areas.

Spiritual Infant

When we first come to know Jesus and are born again, we can be classified as a spiritual infant, lacking knowledge. 1 Peter 2:2 says, "As newborn babes, desire the sincere milk of the word, that you may grow thereby." All that a new Christian desires is milk—that is, nourishment. In the same way that we expect a newborn child to be selfish and demanding, a spiritual infant is only thinking of being fed. The same way that we accept the crying and demanding behavior of a child, we can expect that a new Christian will simply demand spiritual nourishment.

Spiritual Child

As time goes on, the infant becomes a child, who is still focused on self, yet growing. 1 Thessalonians 2:11 says, "As you know how we exhorted and comforted and charged every one of you as a father does his children." The apostle Paul writes that he dealt with the believers as a father deals with children. A child that is just beginning to walk is going to fall and sometimes get hurt. The wise parent does not tell the child to stop walking but encourages and challenges the child to keep growing. A toddler is messy and easily distracted, requiring the constant attention of a parent to avoid trouble. The same applies to a spiritual toddler. The verse talks about comfort, exhortation, and challenge, which help the spiritual child to understand that growing up in Christ takes work.

Spiritual Young Adult

A spiritual young adult begins to change the focus from self to the kingdom of God. 1 John 2:14 says, "I have written... Unto you, young men, because you are strong, and the word of God abides in you, and you have overcome the wicked one." These are believers that have already met some challenges and won some battles. They have overcome obstacles in their lives and have become strong. They have learned to treasure the word of God in their hearts in order to have direction and wisdom for living. These are ready to serve.

Spiritual Parents

The young adult eventually becomes a parent, when he/she feels the desire to help others come to Christ. A spiritual parent is an intentional disciple-maker. This has its challenges. Paul wrote to the Galatians in Galatians 4:19, "My little children, of whom I travail in birth again until Christ be formed in you." Paul compares the work of making new disciples to giving birth. Giving birth is a painful and bloody process, and it takes a special kind of courage to go through it, knowing what it will cost.

In the same manner, if we want to make disciples as Jesus said, we have to realize that it is a painful process. It requires helping others to the point of personal sacrifice, suffering with them and for them, as they go through the first challenges of a newborn baby. There is the fear that possibly this child will not survive to maturity, or that the new disciple will reject the unselfish love of the disciple-maker. The relationship may never be a relationship of friend to friend, but of a parent to a child, meaning that the new convert always will expect things from the spiritual parent without giving anything back. Not easy.

Spiritual Grandparent

Eventually a believer may get to the place where he or she is a spiritual grandparent, where the disciples are now making disciples. Paul challenged Timothy to do just that in 2 Timothy 2:2, saying "and the things that you have heard of me among many witnesses, the same commit to faithful men, who shall be able to teach others also."

Success in growing a church will come when leaders can make disciples that make disciples... and so on. This is the same way that a family grows and becomes a tribe or a nation. This is the plan that Jesus had when He commanded us to make disciples of all nations.

Setting Up a Discipleship System

For a child to grow up into an adult successfully, it requires many things from the environment. God has established the family as a place for children to grow up. A family is a safe yet challenging environment in which to grow. The church is such a family to the spiritual infant. Leaders of the church have to intentionally set up a process so that new converts can become mature disciples.

In His work with his disciples, Jesus used a very successful method. First of all, He spent a lot of time with his disciples—they traveled together for three and a half years. As they traveled, the disciples heard teaching and experienced new things with their master. This is a pattern that we need to follow in the church today. The method that Jesus used applies across all cultures and times. It would be a mistake to think that we can improve on what Jesus did, but that is basically what we have attempted to do traditionally in the church.

Unfortunately, our focus has been on programs where people come together for a special event. Much effort and money are spent in putting together such events so that people will have an experience. This is not discipleship. Discipleship is done through an intimate relationship that develops over time. The focus on experiences is empty without the context of a relationship and ongoing teaching. The experiences must be incorporated into a body of knowledge for them to be effective in shaping disciples.

The church needs to focus on making sure that every mature believer understands the job of a disciple-maker and is fully prepared to share their life and their knowledge in a long-term relationship. This is going to require a new kind of thinking and much love and sacrifice on the part of Christians toward those they desire to disciple.

A discipleship system is a series of teachings and experiences that are prepared so that new converts may grow healthy. Experiences such as baptism, being filled with the Holy Spirit, intense moments of worship, intercessory prayer, and others become powerful within the context of a relationship and by teaching on their meaning. There are many people that have an experience in a crusade or decide to be baptized, but are never seen again because they had no understanding of what had occurred, and there was no one close that could guide them.

The book of Acts, chapter 2:42-47, gives the pattern of the Apostolic church. There is an emphasis on fellowship, continuing daily, breaking bread from house to house, and eating food with gladness. This focus on relationship among believers helped them to grow and become mature.

An example of the general flow of a discipleship system would be something like:

- Events to bring in first-time visitors
- Visitor follow-up
- Connection to a small group or person
- Study of the Bible
- Growth in spiritual gifts
- Service opportunity
- Leadership in service
- Ministry development

All the details of special events, small groups, and Bible studies depend on the decisions of the pastor and leaders. The key principle is to develop resources that will connect with the community rather than just following the preferences of leadership or copying some other church or pastor.

Retention of Converts

One last term that is important to ministry is *retention*. This refers to the ability of the church to keep first-time visitors, have them assimilate into the church, become disciples, and eventually move on to become ministers. Working to improve retention will close the back door of the church.

People will leave the church for various reasons, and some of them are beyond our control.[27] A change in jobs, a major change in life situation, marriage, a poor fit, etc. No matter how godly a minister may be, he will not be able to pastor everyone. There are some people that will grow better and be able to serve God more effectively under another pastor. This is a hard pill to swallow because we don't want anyone to leave our church. However, there are times that we need to let people go graciously, without condemnation, and with a thankful heart that they are continuing in the church.

However, there are some instances where people leave for reasons that can be avoided or dealt with, if we are prepared to understand them.

Some people will leave because of sin, even though they may state other reasons. An axiom obscurely attributed to Blaise Pascal[28] states that people prefer to live in congruence between their beliefs and their behavior. If they are not able to alter their behavior to fit their beliefs, then amazingly they will change their beliefs to fit their behavior. Thus, if someone is living in an ungodly way and cannot change, then they will change their beliefs and adjust to sin in order to have peace in their minds. These people will leave the church no matter what you do, and they will never really state the reason why they leave.

What the church can do is to maintain a culture of grace so that those that leave for this reason can return. This is why it is good not to do an exit interview, because people will never tell you that they're leaving because of sin but will find some other reasons. For them to come back, they would have to take back all those other reasons, which might be very difficult or shameful.

People also leave because of a bad experience with someone in the church, a leader, or even the pastor. It is impossible to avoid bad experiences from affecting people in church, but the leadership can create a culture of forgiveness and reconciliation. All bad experiences have to be dealt with immediately as they happen, or they become more serious and hurtful.

People may leave the church because of isolation. If they are not assimilated and don't make friends within a month or two, chances are they will not stay in the church. Everyone needs relationship and responsibility, or to use simpler terms, everyone needs a friend and a job. The church can create fun events where people can relate to one another informally, establish service teams where people can serve the community and the church, and develop a small group system where believers can connect to one another at home.

In spite of our best efforts, there will come a time when people will choose to leave our church for good or bad reasons. It is best at that point to let them go and pray that they will be able to continue in their walk with the Lord.

Questions

1. Which of the three concepts discussed in this chapter needs to be improved the most in your church: assimilation, discipleship, or retention?

2. What will you do in the next three months to improve your way of doing things?

3. Do you have a plan for discipleship that is written down and known to all? If not, make a decision to work on developing such a plan with your church leadership in the next three months.

4. How fresh is your love for souls? Will you commit to praying: "Lord, increase my love for the souls you have placed in my care"?

Chapter 6: Discipleship and Church Growth

The Correct Perspective on Numbers

Although this is not a book on church growth, this topic cannot be neglected in a book for pastors. Some pastors err by exaggerating one of the following contrasting views concerning numbers:

- Numbers don't matter; what matters is that the church is producing quality disciples.
- It is all about the numbers; anything is ok as long as more people show up to church.

Both views taken to the extreme are wrong and will cause an imbalance in the work of the church. Numbers are important to God, who charged His church to reach the whole world. But producing solid disciples was a large part of the work of Jesus during his years of ministry on the earth. And in fact, as we will see below, making disciples is the only way that the world can be reached.

The truth is that good disciples will produce solid growth, if both the quality of discipleship and larger numbers are part of the vision. In human beings, having two eyes provides stereo vision, which is better than having mono vision (one eye). It is the same here; looking at *discipleship* and *growth* together will provide a stereo vision of the church, helping the pastor reach more people effectively.

The Acts 2 Church

There are many competing ideas and activities that can be done to enhance *either* discipleship or large numbers, to the detriment of the other. But perhaps a good starting point would be to study what the early church did in Acts 2.

> *And they continued stedfastly in the apostles' doctrine and fellowship, and in breaking of bread, and in prayers.*
>
> *And fear came upon every soul: and many wonders and signs were done by the apostles.*
>
> *And all that believed were together, and had all things common;*
>
> *And sold their possessions and goods, and parted them to all men, as every man had need.*
>
> *And they, continuing daily with one accord in the temple, and breaking bread from house to house, did eat their meat with gladness and singleness of heart,*
>
> *Praising God, and having favour with all the people. And the Lord added to the church daily such as should be saved. Acts 2:42-47*

This passage gives a glimpse of the activities of the Apostolic church. Let's list several things: what the church did, the results, and what God did.

What the church did:

- Continued in the Apostles' doctrine
- Continued with fellowship (eating together at home)
- Continued in prayer (daily)
- Demonstrated unity among believers
- Shared material resources (Acts 4:32-37)
- Praised God

The results were:

- Signs and wonders
- Fear upon souls
- Favor from the people

What God did:

- God added souls to the church (Acts 2:41, 4:4, 5:14).

We can estimate that by Acts 6, possibly a few years after Pentecost, the church numbered over 8,000 believers in Jerusalem and surrounding areas. If we want to get those kinds of results, then we need to follow the Apostolic pattern closely, the same way we follow the Apostolic doctrine.

Growth of the Early Church

Jesus commanded his disciples to make disciples:

> *Go ye therefore, and <u>teach</u> all nations, baptizing them in the name of the Father, and of the Son, and of the Holy Ghost:*
>
> *<u>Teaching</u> them to observe all things whatsoever I have commanded you: and, lo, I am with you alway, even unto the end of the world. Amen. Matthew 28:19-20*

The word *teach* (verse 19) in the King James translation is the Greek word *matheteuo*, which is best defined as "to become a pupil; transitively, to disciple." On the other hand, the word *teaching* (verse 20), comes from the Greek *didasko*, which implies a teaching process. Other translations (Young, Darby, NAS, etc.) use the word *disciple* in verse 20, with the sense of "go make disciples." The manner of reaching the world is by way of making disciples who are taught the principles and are guided to apply them by the master (or rabbi). These disciples in turn make other disciples.

Paul charged his disciple, Timothy, to follow exactly that pattern:

> *And the things that thou hast heard of me among many witnesses, the same commit thou to faithful men, who shall be able to teach others also. 2 Timothy 2:2*

In his chapter on "First-Century Disciple-Making Culture," Stan Gleason writes

> "...disciple-making and relationship building gradually diminished and were replaced with an easier and less cumbersome paradigm of

edifice- and personality-driven worship events."[29] The most unfortunate result of the loss of the disciple-making process is that the church has not reached the world. Its growth stagnated by the third century and has never recovered. This is because we have abandoned the commandment of Jesus on making disciples and the Apostolic pattern of growing the church.

Rodney Stark, an American sociologist of religion, writes in *The Triumph of Christianity*[30] that the early church grew from Pentecost (33 AD) to 350 AD at an average rate of 3.4% per year. He calculates this number starting from 1,000 in 33 AD to 6 million by 300 AD, and over 30 million by 350 AD. The 30+ million Christians estimate has long been accepted as valid for a Roman empire where more than half of its residents were Christians. The total population of the Roman empire around that time is believed to have been around 60 million. The 3.4% average growth rate per year also fits several other number milestones estimated by scholars.

However, a growth rate of 3.4% is not very impressive, although it reached millions three hundred years later. What was the growth rate in the first few years of the gospel, the Apostolic growth rate? We can do a calculation based on some numbers from the Bible.

Stark begins with 1,000 on the day of Pentecost, not quite believing that 3,000 were added on that day. For the sake of comparison, we can start with that figure, and assume that enough were won on the day of Pentecost to bring the total to 3,000 (Acts 2:41). Sometime later, another 5,000 were added (just men, Acts 4:4). Just before Stephen died in Acts 7 (36 AD,[31]) we can estimate the size of the church very conservatively as at least 8,120 plus. Based on these numbers for a three-year period, the average growth rate for the church was 100%. This is basically a growth rate where numbers are doubled every year (100% growth). If the church had maintained this growth rate, it would have reached 30 million in fifteen years, or by the year 51 AD instead of 350 AD.

The Apostolic pattern to reach the world is by making disciples that make disciples.

If each disciple can produce another disciple every year, the church could win the whole world in less than thirty years, even if it started with a small number. See the following section on the Math of Discipleship.

The discipleship process for growth is successful in the context of an Acts 2 church. We see the following elements: doctrine and prayer are emphasized, ministry takes place in the homes, resources are shared to help the poor, God confirms the work by signs and wonders, and He adds to the church the multitudes that will be saved.

The Math of Discipleship

As a result of the math of discipleship, the church today could win the whole world in less than thirty years starting with just twenty believers, if we did discipleship following the pattern of the Apostolic church. This means making the following changes to our churches to match the Apostolic pattern:

Chapter 6: Discipleship and Church Growth

Churches today	Apostolic church
Focus activities on a temple	No building, focus on the homes
Invite people to a temple for an event	Reach people at home for ministry
Focus on programs and activities	Focus on discipleship
Ministry done by specialists	Ministry done by all believers
Use financial resources to pay for building and staff	Use financial resources to help the poor

Example: Suppose there are twenty believers in one church and each wins one disciple every year. The new disciples likewise win a disciple per year and so on. Look at the following growth numbers. Note especially the results by year 29!

Year 1: 40
Year 2: 80
Year 3: 160
Year 4: 320
Year 5: 640
Year 6: 1,280
Year 7: 2,560
Year 8: 5,120
Year 9: 10,240
Year 10: 20,480
Year 11: 41,000
Year 12: 82,000
Year 13: 164,000

Year 14: 328,000
Year 15: 656,000
Year 16: 1.3 million
Year 17: 2.6 million
Year 18: 5.2 million
Year 19: 10.4 million
Year 20: 20.8 million
Year 21: 41 million
Year 22: 82 million
Year 23: 164 million
Year 24: 328 million
Year 25: 656 million
Year 26: 1.3 billion
Year 27: 2.6 billion
Year 28: 5.2 billion
Year 29: 10.4 billion*

*Note: The world population in 2019 is estimated at 7.7 billion, and it is generally believed that it will remain stable around that number for the early part of the twenty-first century.

The calculation above shows that any small group of twenty Christians could win the world in less than thirty years through the discipleship method.

What would happen if even just a fraction of today's Christians would decide to focus on discipleship, say 2 million believers worldwide? Starting with 2 million, in eleven years we would have over 8 billion Christians. Again, that is more than the estimated world population.

Of course, these calculations are only estimates, since not everyone would believe the gospel. But the point is that we have the potential to reach everyone alive on the earth with the gospel, and allow them to choose, in eleven years or less, if we would focus on discipleship worldwide.

The question then is, why don't we follow the Apostolic pattern? The answer is that we have inherited a flawed system of church structure and function from centuries of church practice, with a focus on the performance of a few (priests) in a location (temple) at a specific time in the week (Sunday). This focus is very far from the commandment of Jesus and the Apostolic pattern, and it must be changed completely if we are to win the world.

Does God Want a Temple?

One question that must be considered is, how important is having a temple for church growth? Having a building is convenient and useful for any meetings and events of the body. However, the larger share of the finances of any church goes into paying for a building that is used just a few hours a week. We tend to forget that the Apostolic church grew explosively without a dedicated temple. Initially, they met in the Jewish temple for prayer, but after the miracle of the lame man and persecution from the priests and the religious establishment, they could not meet in the Jewish temple.

We may think that not having a temple for meetings was a detriment to the early church, when in fact, it may have been an asset! Perhaps the church is more effective without owning a temple? Certainly, the growth of believers happens outside of the temple, in the places where they live and function. Many people show up as Christians on Sunday morning, but it is what they do outside of the temple during the week that proves their Christianity.

George Barna and Frank Viola write in their controversial book *Pagan Christianity*[32] that the early Christian church met in homes all over the Roman empire. It was not until the third century that the church began to meet in the formerly pagan temples emptied by decree of the Emperor Justinian in 389 AD. There is no mention in the Bible of a building for any of the churches mentioned, but there are references to churches meeting in houses in several places (See Romans 16:5, 1 Corinthians 16:9, Colossians 4:15, Philemon 2). I have written more on this topic of God's view of a temple elsewhere.[33]

If the Apostolic church grew without a temple, ministering from house to house with a focus on discipleship, perhaps it is a mistake to think that we can improve on the Apostolic pattern by purchasing larger and larger buildings. We cannot win the world by focusing church life on a building, programming evangelism as an event, and having ministry done by specialists, instead of following the pattern of the early church and the discipleship principles commanded by Jesus!

Current Church Growth Numbers

Using information from chapter 10 and appendix IV, we can compare the growth of a church that is growing by regular programming (say 15% a year) to the growth produced by the discipleship method described above.

As before, we start with twenty believers that are willing to work.

	Discipleship (100% growth)	Programs (15% growth)
Initial	20	20
Year 5	640	40
Year 10	20,840	81

It can be seen that there is not much competition. The discipleship method is overwhelmingly superior in the long run.

Naturally, there are several assumptions that would make these numbers different in real life. For example, there will be some loss because not all the disciples would stay, and some may even pass away. In addition, other factors may hinder achieving 100% duplication of the numbers of disciples every year. However, there are other factors on the plus side: a disciple may quickly bring in close family members, children, etc., so any loss for the reasons stated above may be offset.

Even with those considerations, the discipleship method is clearly superior. If these numbers do not make any pastor drop all the programs and concentrate on discipleship, I don't know what will!

Questions

1. Does your church have an intentional focus on discipleship? Why or why not?

2. What is the greatest hindrance in your situation to developing a strong discipleship focus? What will you do in the next three months to change it?

3. Do the math: Write down the number of members that would be willing to make one disciple in the next twelve months. Then double that number for ten years and so on. At what point would you reach all the people in your city or community? Let that vision motivate you to do the work.

LEADERSHIP

Chapter 7: Focus on the Leader

"Leadership is the process of influencing others to work toward a mutually desired vision." David Burkus.

John Maxwell's ubiquitous definition of leadership has been modified several times, but I like the version above by David Burkus. There is an emphasis on vision as the end result of good leadership. This concept is a large part of Aubrey Malphurs' definition of leadership in the Christian context: "... a godly servant (character) who knows and sees where he or she is going (mission and vision) and has followers (influence)."[34]

In the Christian realm, the result of leadership is disciples who are growing in their spiritual life and their service to God, and who are making other disciples.

Knowledge of Self

In order to lead others, leaders need to learn about themselves. The ability to lead depends on the leader's understanding of himself, as seen by those that are lead. There are three different things to consider: character, abilities, and experience.

By *character* I mean our preferred mode of functioning internally and in social situations. *Abilities* are skills we possess which may be applied in leading a group of people. *Experiences* are those instances where we have been successful in the past, or where we have failed and have learned from the failure.

Character Analysis

There are many character analyses and personality tests that can offer information about ourselves. Depending on their design, they will give information about our preferences and behavior in social or institutional situations. Many of them are used by large corporations as part of staff development programs. Most personality tests can be taken online for a small fee and will provide a report. Following is a synopsis of the more common ones, followed by a longer treatment of the Myers-Briggs Personality Inventory.

16PF

The 16 Personality Factor Questionnaire[35] is designed to measure normal behaviors and can be used for career development and counseling. It measures character qualities like warmth, reasoning, emotional stability, dominance, rule-consciousness, social boldness, sensitivity, apprehension, openness to change, and others. This is used often for career counseling and job placement.

The Big Five (Five Factor Model, NEO Personality Inventory)

J. M. Digman proposed that personalities are built on five factors: Openness, Conscientiousness, Extraversion, Agreeableness, and Neuroticism.[36] These five personality traits explain why people react differently in the same situation. Steven Kessler recently wrote a clearly accessible approach to self-analysis using this theory.[37] The Five Factor Model and the NEO Personality Inventory have been used by career professionals and psychologists for recruitment and candidate assessment and have proved helpful in cross-cultural studies.[38]

Keirsey Temperament Assessment

David Keirsey enhanced the temperament theory that was originally devised by Hippocrates and Plato, which suggests four general personality types: artisan, guardian, idealist, and rational.[39] Keirsey then divided the four temperaments into two categories and two types, ending with sixteen personality types very similar to those in the Myers-Briggs personality type inventory described below.

Myers-Briggs Type Indicator

One assessment that has been helpful to many people personally and socially is the Myers-Briggs Type Indicator. Katharine Briggs and Isabel Briggs Myers developed a system of personality analysis based on the work of Carl Jung.[40] They present four dimensions of personality to help us understand our preferences in thinking and behaving. Our focus can be either:

- E or I: People and things (*Extraversion*) or ideas and information (*Introversion*).
  This has to do with the way we direct and receive energy, to/from the outside (E) or to/from the inside (I).
- S or I: Facts and reality (*Sensing*) or possibilities and potential (*Intuition*).
  This relates to the way we take in information, real and tangible (S) or big picture and patterns (I).
- T or F: Logic and fruits (*Thinking*) or values and relationship (*Feeling*).

This has to do with the way we make decisions and come to conclusions, either based on logic and objectivity (T) or based on personal and social values (F).
- J or P: A lifestyle that is structured (*Judgment*) or one that goes with the flow (*Perception*).
  This is the way we approach the outside world, either with decisiveness and closure (J) or with flexibility and spontaneity (P).

The combination of the four preferences using letters becomes our personality type, for example, ESPJ or INTF. There are sixteen different personality types and, based on research, there is an associated phrase that describes the salient feature of each personality type.

For example, INFJ (a person that is introverted, intuitive, feeling, and judging) is described as "the Counselor" type. Other personality types also have descriptors as shown below, and in appendix II:

ESFJ: The Provider
ESTJ: The Supervisor
ENFJ: The Giver
INFP: The Idealist
ESFP: The Performer

Although God is able to use any personality type, this analysis can help us to understand our personal tendencies and how we can best function as leaders. For example, an extrovert can naturally function as a leader with people, but this does not mean that an introvert cannot be a good leader. A good leader should be able to function as an intuitive, meaning someone that can envision the future in an intuitive manner; on the other hand, the sensate function is important in order to be grounded in the present. A good leader should be able to function as a thinker, but not at the expense of disregarding important feelings in himself and his followers. Finally, a leader should know when to bring things to a close, using good judgment; however, there are times to consider different options, and to be open to perceive all the possibilities.

We can look at different leaders in the Bible and easily assign to them some of the Myers-Briggs descriptors based on what we read. For example, Moses was probably an introvert; he was so comfortable by himself in the desert, that after years, he found it difficult to communicate. To help him, God had to appoint his brother Aaron to speak for him.

For David, we can assign the descriptor of *feeling* to his personality type, as he is able to touch our hearts through his writings even today. The apostle John had a nurturing personality (ISFJ), and he wrote much about disciples loving each other as Jesus loves.

The personal applications of understanding my personality type are many. For example, if I am an *introvert*, I understand that I need to make special efforts to relate to the people I lead. If I am an *intuitive* or a *sensate*, I need to understand how to communicate with followers of the opposite type. If I prefer *thinking* or *feeling*, I have to allow for followers who may fall in the opposite dimension and not disregard their contributions. Finally, I should understand that it is important to bring projects to a close (*judgment*), but also there are times that all possibilities need to be considered (*perceiving*).

One can take a simple online survey to determine personality type and learn further applications to personal life and the church work environment.

Abilities

What are my strengths and weaknesses? If we are not aware of both of these, it is possible to make great mistakes with implications not only for ourselves but for the church. One way to discover and capitalize on personal strengths is by taking a different type of assessment.

Gallup's Strengths Finder

Over the past few decades, the Gallup research group has studied how talent is applied to many different roles from housekeepers to chief executives. They have found some harmful myths about personal development. Two common ones are the ideas that "you can be whatever you want to be" and that "you will grow the most by improving your weak areas." The truth is that you really cannot be anything you want to be, there may be physical or mental limitations; however, you can be better at being who you are. Secondly, their studies show that you will grow the most by focusing on your strengths and finding ways to complement your weaknesses.

The Gallup researchers found that most people have core personality traits that are stable throughout adulthood. The most successful people start with a dominant talent and then add skills, knowledge, and practice to become greater. They defined *strengths* as the ability to consistently provide outstanding performance. A strength is a combination of a talent (a natural way of thinking, feeling, or behaving) and investment (time spent practicing, developing skills, and increasing knowledge).

In the book *Strengths Finder 2.0*,[41] Tom Rath lists thirty-four possible strength themes that may form the core of your personality. Among them are, for example, Activator, Deliberative,

Futuristic, Includer, Maximizer, Relator, Strategic, and so on. The main idea of this research is that you will be the most effective and fulfilled when you operate in your areas of strength and concentrate on developing it.

The Clifton Strengths Finder assessment, which can be taken online, will order the thirty-four strengths themes for you from strongest to weakest. Gallup researchers suggest that the top five themes are the strengths that you should focus on and develop for personal fulfillment and success.

The assessment will also organize your *strengths set* into one of four domains, which are important when working in a team:

Executing: people with dominant executing themes make things happen.
Influencing: people with dominant influencing themes take charge, speak up, and make sure others are heard.
Relationship Building: people with dominant relationship building themes build strong relationships that hold the team together and help it function best.
Strategic Thinking: people with dominant strategic thinking themes absorb and analyze information for better decision-making.

Once you understand your *strengths* and which is your preferred *domain*, you should act to maximize your potential by making small changes in your work in the church. Secondly, watch out for blind spots, and find people or processes to complement your weak areas.

Experience

Our past experiences shape our current thinking and behavior to a great extent. Rather than responding to every new person and situation as something new, we tend to think in categories. Once we can assign the present experience to a category, without realizing it, we tend to respond according to what happened in the past. This way of acting can cause many problems and complicate our communication and behavior unnecessarily.

For example, we may respond with anger to a comment that was meant as a positive criticism, simply because someone else in our past used the same phrases to wound us. In that instance, we are responding to a hurt from the past and are not relating to the person in the present.

Emotional Intelligence

Emotional Intelligence is the ability to understand our emotions and identify them in other people in such a way that our feelings don't get in the way of good relationships.

Travis Bradberry and Jean Graves[42] have written extensively on this subject, working as consultants for many global companies and testing over half a million subjects to measure their Emotional Quotient (EQ).

Besides conducting research, they also have developed a process and strategies to help people improve their emotional intelligence. Their studies show that EQ has a great impact on the success of people, perhaps even more than the IQ. Of all the people they studied at work, they found that 90% of high performers were also high in EQ. On the opposite side, just 20% of low performers were high in EQ.

Chapter 7: Focus on the Leader

Half of emotional intelligence deals with Personal Competence: Self-Awareness and Self-Management. The other half deals with Social Competence: Social Awareness, and Relationship Management. Following are definitions of these terms:

Self-Awareness: the ability to correctly perceive my emotions in the moment and understand my tendencies across situations. It includes knowing my typical reactions to specific events, challenges, and people.

Self-Management: the ability to use awareness of my emotions to choose my behavior in the moment. This means managing my emotional reactions to situations and people.

Social Awareness: the ability to correctly pick up on emotions in other people and understand what is going on with them. This includes perceiving what others are thinking and feeling even if I do not agree.

Relationship Management: the ability to use awareness of my own emotions and those of people around me to manage interactions successfully. This will achieve clear communication and effective handling of conflict. It builds on the other three emotional intelligence skills above.

Bradberry and Graves believe that everyone can increase their emotional intelligence and refined sixty-six strategies for those that want to do so. Among them are:

- Quit Treating Your Feelings as Good or Bad
- Observe the Ripple Effect from Your Emotions
- Know Who and What Pushes Your Buttons
- Keep a Journal about Your Emotions
- Visit Your Values
- Spot Your Emotions in Books, Movies, Music
- Seek Feedback
- Get to Know Yourself under Stress

Increasing emotional intelligence can be as simple as asking someone close to us, like a spouse for instance, about our reactions in times of stress. Growth in EQ requires a serious and humble approach, but the results will be worth the work.

Leaders must have good emotional intelligence to guide others and to be able to manage their own feelings and responses in a positive way. Fortunately, this is something that can be developed with attention and some effort.

Time Management

One of the hidden but necessary abilities of a successful leader is good use of time. Since we all have twenty-four hours in a day, why do some people seem to get much more accomplished? The answer is obviously that some manage their time better than others. As pastors, we are pressured by church work, personal life, and family activities. If we don't manage our time wisely, we will always be late, stressed, and grumpy! We have to learn to differentiate between the important and the urgent.

In *The Renegade Pastor's Guide to Time Management*,[43] Nelson Searcy discusses the importance of pastors being effective (achieving goals) and efficient (using minimum effort). He outlines some practices that help pastors succeed, including having a regular day of rest (Sabbath), getting up one hour earlier, timing routine activities to improve efficiency, keeping a single calendar, writing ideas and tasks, being willing to delegate, using technology wisely, making the most of meetings, and turning wait time into useful time.

For example, in order to be more efficient and effective, I recently retooled the way we organize the cell groups in our church. In the past, we met once a week to pass out the lesson outline for the week and for me to teach the lessons to the group leaders. Due to the time this required, it left little time in our weekly meetings for leadership training and motivation. Having a second meeting proved impractical—everyone's too busy. And then, there was always someone that missed the meeting and needed a synopsis, and there were always people that lost their paper for the week and had to bother somebody (pastor or pastor's assistant) to get another copy.

All this turmoil has been circumvented by two simple practices using technology. First, instead of teaching the lesson live during our meeting, I make a video of it and post it online. That way, everyone can access it on their own time and hear the information more than once, if necessary. We don't have to do any more special synopses personally or on the phone. In addition, through a collaborative effort, all group leaders obtained a ten-inch tablet, and their lesson outlines are emailed directly to their tablets. We don't have to make copies at all! We also preloaded the tablets with a plethora of Bible studies, special lessons, and other resources for the group leaders. Voila! Now I can devote my time during our leadership meetings to leadership!

How can we focus our time on what is really important? In the *7 Habits of Highly Effective People*,[44] Steven Covey mentions four quadrants of time along the axes of *urgent-not urgent* and *important-not important*. There are a few things that are urgent and important, but many that are urgent and not important, or neither. Our focus should be on what is urgent and important, and on what is important. Things in the important quadrant include planning, prevention, and improvement. Focus on this quadrant will prevent many things from becoming crises (urgent) and causing us to lose our focus for the day.

Often, we are guilted into doing something because someone else has a crisis (urgent, not important) that they dump in our laps. I remember the time that someone called me on a Monday night with a marriage crisis, just as I was heading out the door with my wife for some time alone. This was a couple that I had already been counseling and they really had not put forth much effort. Rather than running to meet them, I told them I had another appointment and could not see them that night, but to pray and follow the steps we had discussed earlier in our conversations. When I called them the next day, they had worked things out themselves, and I congratulated myself on making a hard decision at the time. Needless to say, my wife was happy.

Morten Hansen writes in *Great at Work*[45] that the key to top performance is not the amount of work, but work that is *focused* and *relevant* to the most important goals. He describes that people's motivation are based on the marriage of passion and purpose. Although pastors generally benefit from both, we need to focus more closely on all the activities of pastoring to discover exactly where our passion and purpose connect with our strengths. Hansen writes that we can all learn to work smarter, not just harder, and achieve more by implementing some key principles. Among these principles are "do less, then obsess," "redesign your work," "don't just learn, loop," "fight and unite," and "use collaboration wisely."

Now What?

These are all great ideas, but useless to us unless we decide to take action right away. Many times, as pastors, we feel that we are accomplishing a lot because we are very busy, but we need to look at our activities to make sure that we are staying focused. There are people and pleasures that are a great sink of time and energy—we should avoid those at all costs! Likewise, a serious look at our weekly and monthly calendars would help to identify areas of improvement. Learning about our strengths, as pointed out earlier in this chapter, and then focusing our work on those areas will increase our effectiveness, efficiency, and enjoyment as we serve God.

Questions

1. Have you taken a personality analysis test? If not, do a search online and take one according to your preference. Consider the Myers Briggs test.

2. What have you discovered or confirmed about yourself by taking the personality test? How will that impact the way you work as a leader in your church?

3. Are you aware of your personal strengths? If not, invest in a thorough analysis of your strengths and put your strengths to work.

4. Have you identified the weaknesses in your abilities? How will you find other team members that will complement those weaknesses so that the team will have success?

5. Sometimes we focus too much on our past experiences. But what worked in the past may not work today, as the world is changing too quickly. Are you willing to let go of your past successes, understanding that *what got you here won't get you there*?

6. How satisfied are you with the way you organize your time? What changes can you make this week to make your days more effective and efficient?

Chapter 8: More on Leadership

There are many concepts that would help leaders to grow above the average, but in this chapter, I have chosen only three topics to emphasize:

- the Importance of Vision for a Church,
- the Necessity of Communicating Vision Well, and
- the Ability to Make Good Decisions.

Vision is needed to have a clear direction in the church. Then that vision must be communicated in a clear and compelling way. Good decisions by the leadership will move the church toward the vision.

The Importance of Vision for a Church

Vision is the ability to imagine a future desired by a person or a group. In the context of the church, it is the ability to imagine a future in the will of God, where good things desired come into being. The final vision of a Christian is, of course, a new life in heaven, where according to John, there will be no more tears, sorrow or crying, pain or death (Revelations 21:4). A temporal vision on the journey to that final vision is a future where family members are blessed, material needs are supplied, illness is banished, good health and spiritual joy are daily blessings, and many more have come to follow Jesus.

So how can we conceive a vision consistent with these visions in a fallen world populated by hurt and broken people? How can we imagine something so powerfully that it becomes the motivation for people to work and sacrifice? Amazingly, it seems that we have been made for such a task.

Man's imagination is unique among all created beings. Imagination is the first step in the process of creation. Before some *thing* can come into existence, it must first be envisioned (imagined), and its benefits deemed worthwhile enough to motivate the Creator to work. Genesis 1:26 says that man was created in God's image. At that point, the most important attribute of God shown was His creative ability. That creative ability was given to man, and in fact, the first work that man did was to give a unique name to every living creature.

> *And out of the ground the Lord God formed every beast of the field, and every fowl of the air; and brought them unto Adam to see what he would call them: and whatsoever <u>Adam called every living creature</u>, that was the name thereof. Genesis 2:19*

This is important because it shows man using language in a creative way, the same way God used language to create the universe in Genesis 1. Thus, man was copying what God had done, showing that he was a fit inheritor of the Creator.

Besides giving man the ability to be creative in the physical world, God also granted man a gift that until then had only been the prerogative of the Creator: the ability to create spiritual life. Man was allowed to create other beings that would have eternity in their hearts: children. There is no indication in the Bible that either angels or the enemy is able to create other spiritual beings. Was this the reason for Satan's jealousy and hate for mankind? It is also interesting to note that this ability will only be ours while men are living on the earth (Luke 20:35).

The ability to *imagine* and the freedom to use it for good or evil was mentioned by God as He made a choice to wipe humanity from the face of the earth, and later to confound their tongue.

> *And God saw that the wickedness of man was great in the earth, and that every <u>imagination of the thoughts</u> of his heart was only evil continually. Genesis 6:5*
>
> *And the LORD said, I will destroy man whom I have created from the face of the earth; both man, and beast, and the creeping thing, and the fowls of the air; for it repenteth me that I have made them. Genesis 6:7*
>
> *And the Lord said, behold, the people is one, and they have all one language; and this they begin to do: and now nothing will be restrained from them which they have <u>imagined to do</u>. Genesis 11:5*

So we have been uniquely crafted by God with the power to imagine the future and to make ourselves and our environment conform to that imagination. We live in an imagined world. Look around at all the wonderful advances of science, medicine, and communication that have taken place in the last fifty years. This is a display of the ability of mankind to imagine and create granted to him by his Creator God.

God gave Abraham a great vision of his future where his descendants would populate all the land he could see from a mountaintop. God later added that his descendants would be as many as the stars.

> *Lift up now thine eyes, and look from the place where thou art northward, and southward, and eastward, and westward: For <u>all the land</u> which thou seest, to thee will I give it, and to thy seed for ever.*
>
> *And I will make thy seed as the dust of the earth: so that if a man can number the dust of the earth, then shall thy seed also be numbered. Genesis 13:14-16*
>
> *And he brought him forth abroad, and said, Look now toward heaven, and tell <u>the stars</u>, if thou be able to number them: and he said unto him, So shall thy seed be. Genesis 15:5*

Paul prays for believers in Ephesus that they would be able to see a vision of how great is the calling of God to share His glory and His power.

> *The <u>eyes of your understanding</u> being enlightened; that ye may know what is the hope of his calling, and what the riches of the glory of his inheritance in the saints, And what is the exceeding greatness of his power toward us who believe, according to the working of his mighty power, Ephesians 1:18-19*

As leaders of God's church, we have to use this magnificent gift to imagine a future for each church within the context of its community and its time. This future will include personal and corporate elements. It must grow from the body, not be imposed from the top. To be effective, it cannot be just a restatement of some Bible verse, although it certainly must be consistent with Scripture. Then as it is written down and communicated, it should unite the congregation to move in the same direction and with the same purpose.

The Necessity of Communicating the Vision Well[46]

Once a vision is clearly and formally established, it is the job of leadership to communicate that vision to the church. The pastor and leaders must be skilled in communicating this vision, otherwise, followers will not be able to connect with it. The following are some key points that need to be considered:

Do the church members understand and believe the vision?

The vision must be presented with the hearers in mind. It cannot be so complicated or deeply theological that people cannot relate to it. The context should either be *a great need* in the community or an unexploited *spiritual opportunity* that God has made available to the church.

The content of the vision matters to the hearers because of the possible impact on their lives and on the community where they live. How exactly will the work of this church change people's lives, and how will the contributions of each member affect the outcome?

The credibility of the vision depends a lot on the leader's integrity and personal life. People need to see that the life of the leader backs up the content of the vision, and that God is uniquely blessing the leader's life and ministry. The leader must have strong gifts or abilities that elicit commitment and dedication in the followers.

Obviously, the leader must be personally dedicated to the cause. His life must demonstrate his commitment to it, and at the same time showcase the power and possibilities in the vision.

Vision Casting – Practical Elements

Many churches present the vision of the church once a year, possibly in January. This is a special time to present to the church a state-of-the-church sermon, which may include a report of past accomplishments and future strategies and goals for the year. This presentation should take advantage of the ideas presented below to enhance communication.

As the leader presents the vision, he must be aware of the people he is communicating with and connect with their needs, dreams, and hopes. The language of communication must be expressive. Telling a story that embodies the vision is more effective and memorable than using only description. Jesus used many stories (parables) to show the principles he wanted to communicate, and they are still remembered today.

One powerful story that should be shared is the leader's personal testimony of the impact of the vision on his own life. The success stories of others, including some in the congregation, can also fuel excitement and belief in the vision.

The use of metaphors and similes, photos, graphics, and logos help to bring a presentation to life. A carefully chosen song can also touch the hearts of people. The leader must speak with conviction and boldness, never wavering in his delivery.

The use of a skit or drama is an effective method to bring to life the vision of the church. This does not require a professional set of actors. People from the congregation will connect well with others and, through their own participation, become more invested in the message.

The vision should be communicated to new members of the church as part of a new-member's class or orientation. It should be part of any brochure that is given to first-time visitors and be part of any communication to the church and the community.

Most vision casters believe that people will forget the vision within one to two months. Therefore, various elements of the vision should be brought before the congregation often for people to remember. Some good times to do this are just before the summer (May) and in the fall (September) when people return from vacation and children return to school.

The Ability to Make Good Decisions

Various writers, most notably Watchman Nee,[47] have written about the soul of man being composed of three functions: Thinking, Feeling, and Choosing (the Will). Much has been written about the importance of our thought life and how to manage our feelings well. However, not as much has been written about the way that we arrive at decisions, how we *choose*. And yet the choices that we make in life very much determine our personal success and those of the people we lead.

We expect leaders to lead by making good timely decisions. In fact, we trust them to do so, understanding that their choices will affect our families and churches for generations.

If leaders had all the information needed and sufficient time to process it using logic, or if God would always clearly direct us, we would always arrive at decisions that would be foolproof. Yet often, the decisions that are most important must be made with incomplete information, under the pressure of time and without a clear divine mandate. The following discussion focuses on the human part of decision-making, but this must be complemented in practice with prayer and steps of faith.

The psychologist Martin Seligman recently wrote that our capacity to build hypotheses about the future may be the defining attribute of human intelligence.[48] He wrote that perhaps a better name for human beings, instead of *Homo sapiens* (Wise Man), might be *Homo prospectus* (Prospecting Man). He believes that man's projective ability enables him not only to contemplate any behavior, but to motivate him through an imagined future reward. He establishes a relationship between prospection, evaluation, emotion, and motivation. This process of prospection (building hypotheses for the choices that we make) allows us to make good decisions even in the face of incomplete information. In order to achieve the desired prospection, man capitalizes on three mechanisms: intuitive guidance (based on emotion, information and experience), deliberative guidance and imaginative guidance.[49] As leaders, our success in *choosing* will depend on intentionally imagining the chain of events along any one choice made, and evaluating the results.

A leader fueled by vision is able to take this personal internal process and share it with a group of people, who will be motivated to work to bring that vision to pass. On the way to the vision, there are many decisions that must be made correctly in order to reach it. It does not matter how wonderful the vision might be, and how well it is communicated, if the leader cannot guide the church toward it. Thus the importance of good decision-making.

Guidance from Above

As Christians, we can depend on God to guide us through difficult decisions. However, we have the responsibility to prepare ourselves to receive that guidance. We are still responsible for choices made when we do not clearly hear a directive from above. Perhaps I am very carnal, but as I made most of the important choices in my life, I did not hear a voice from heaven, have a dream, read a Bible verse with the answer, or receive directions from an angel or a church leader. All of the important decisions I made were with fear and trembling, after much prayer, deliberation, and hesitation. If many things worked out well, it is only because of the grace of God, and His hand guiding me through the Holy Spirit.

The point is that we can improve our decision-making by following a logical process, while always being open to direction from God. This is consistent with what we see in the Word of God concerning God's provision, for example. Jesus said in Matthew 6:25-33 that our heavenly Father will provide for us if we put the kingdom of God first. We understand that this does not mean that we sit around waiting for God to send ravens with food, like He did with the prophet (1 Kings 17:4-6). Rather, we are to work and provide for our household (1 Timothy 5:8; 2 Thessalonians 3:10-11), having faith that God will provide in times when we are not able.

Decision-Making in the Church

Making decisions in a church can be a dangerous process. The great majority of the time, voting as a way of making corporate decisions should be avoided. This is especially important if there has been an open discussion on the topic of the vote, because people will be invested in what they argue for, and there will be winners and losers. Regardless of the result of the vote, the process will lead to some division in the church.

Major decisions should be made by a consensus of leadership and presented to the congregation. The pastor should take care to never shock the congregation. This will not happen if there are discussions with the leadership in private over time.

Even if asked not to speak on the subject of the decision, the leaders will leak the information; it is unavoidable, it is human nature. Rather than trying to fight against this tendency, the pastor can use it to prepare the congregation for the decision.

Now, if the leaders cannot agree on the choice to be made, bringing it to the congregation at that point would only cause further division. My feeling as a pastor has been that if I cannot achieve consensus among the leadership, then it is time to go back and make a different choice or prepare a new plan before going any further.

When working with the leadership group to make a decision, the pastor should be aware that there are some influencers in the congregation that may not be part of the official leadership. Those people need to be considered, and their opinion and contribution requested in private. There is an elderly mother in our congregation that has never held a position of leadership yet has a great deal of influence through her family. I am always careful to include her in leadership discussions of important decisions because her support is needed when we roll out the plan.

In the context of decision-making, I have taught church leadership that there are three types of decisions:

1. The first one derives from a clear biblical mandate. In those cases, we simply follow the teaching of Scripture regardless of the outcome and pray for good success. When informing the leadership and the congregation, the reason for the choice is clearly communicated.
2. The second type of decision does not relate to a biblical principle, and there are options that appear equally righteous. In that case, the pastor and the leadership take time to make the right choice together and then inform the congregation.

3. However, I make it a point to emphasize that if I hear clearly from God at any point in the process, it is my responsibility to inform the leadership about the will of God. This last argument should be used seldom and only with complete confidence, because the future credibility of the pastor rests on the outcome.

The following discussion will focus on the second type of decision-making, where the pastor and leadership have to make a decision together.

Practical Skills in Decision-Making

Simple decisions are straightforward, and their payoff risks are manageable. However, more complex decisions force us to predict the future and may be significantly riskier. This is especially important when the decision affects a group of people, like a church or a community. Most of us tend to overestimate our current influence and underestimate the future impact of our decisions.

Maps, Models, and Influence Diagrams

Steven Johnson, New York Times best-selling author, has written about decision-making[50] and offers some important considerations when making complex decisions.

Complicated decisions require three steps: we make a map of all the possible paths available; we make predictions about where those different paths might lead us; and we reach a decision by considering the outcome of each path versus the desired goal. This kind of process is best done using a hand-drawn map, so that we can clearly visualize the process. At this point, no possible paths should be rejected, even if at first they don't seem as attractive.

Avoid Anchoring and Groupthink

When making difficult decisions, sometimes people have a tendency to predetermine a choice (*anchor*) and change other parameters to adjust to it. This can be a mistake because that anchored choice may be a variable that can be changed to achieve the best outcome.

Diversity in a decision-making group is actually a benefit. Even though it may take longer to reach a consensus, the variety of perspectives will provide a better solution. *Groupthink* is the response to the pressure of the group to conform quickly and avoid the tension that comes with a variety of opinions. However, it can squelch valuable contributions and lead to poor results. As a pastor it is important to avoid communicating a personal preference as deliberations proceed because of the influence that it will have on some members of the leadership team.

Dealing with Unknowns

As deliberations proceed, there are instances where information is not available. These can be classified as *knowable unknowns, inaccessible unknowns*, and *unknowable unknowns*.[51] A leader has to deal with all three of these, and especially evaluate the risks associated with the last category. If it does not pose a great risk to lack certain information, it is put aside for the moment and the process can go on.

Knowable unknowns can be researched to provide the needed information, and *inaccessible unknowns* can turn into *knowable unknowns*, depending on the circumstances and how much time is available for research before making the decision.

Scenario Planning

This part of complex decision-making involves considering the final outcome of a path and engaging the group in a description of that outcome. This is a narrative, creative exercise, where people use their imagination to flesh out a possible future. This type of exercise will help the leadership assess the benefits and risks associated with a particular choice.

Value Model (LVM)

One way to arrive at a complex decision is to prepare a list of important values to the church associated with the choice to be made. These values are then brought into the discussion, and different choices are evaluated as being supportive of those values or harmful to them. By values we mean important principles, most of which may be based on Christian concepts from the Bible or from practical considerations.

A little math can help in this process through the "linear value modeling" (LVM) method. Here, one gives a number to each value based on its importance (on a scale between 0 and 1), and each possible choice is given a percentage based on the possibility of meeting that particular value. These two numbers are multiplied together to give a "value," and all the values are added for a particular choice. The choice with the highest number meets the goal of being consistent with the values of the church.

To see a sample of LVM, see appendix III for its application to the choice of the next step for our church, as we exceeded our capacity in a building.

Risk Magnitude

Any choice that is made has a risk associated with it; that is, at the same time that we gain from the choice we make, we may lose something valuable. As we get closer to making the final choice, we need to consider the possibility of loss. If there is a chance of risking something too valuable, then that particular choice needs to be carefully evaluated and may be discarded.

This kind of analysis forces us to look at something we naturally tend to avoid, the highly unlikely catastrophe. Some outcomes are so disastrous to a church that it's a good idea to avoid them (even if their likelihood is slim) by choosing a safer option.

Small-Risk Trials

As we move further along in our decision-making process and can identify just a few possibilities to choose from, it can be very helpful if we do small-scale trials. Trying different choices on a small scale minimizes the risks associated with them and may give valuable information for implementation. Rather than arguing about the possible benefits and drawbacks of a few choices, a group may do these limited experiments to move forward with valuable information.

For example, if we are trying to decide the method of evangelism to use for the next year, it would be helpful to try various things in a small scale and assess the results. The one or two methods that bring the most visitors to the church should be the ones that we can scale up to involve greater resources or the whole church.

Questions

1. Are you able to state the vision for your church right now? Test your leaders to see if they are able to do that. If not, there is some vision work that needs to be done.

2. Are you intentionally programming times in your church calendar to rekindle vision? If not, place it in your calendar in a formal way, then celebrate and dream together.

3. How would you rate your skills in decision-making: average, poor, or excellent? What will you do, based

on your reading here, to improve the quality of your decisions?

MANAGEMENT

Chapter 9: Church Structure and Church Systems

Church Structure

All churches have a structure, whether intentional or as a result of historical events. By structure we mean how people are organized in order to work together. Since the structure determines effectiveness, it is best to organize the church intentionally. That is, not simply to repeat the organization we have seen in the past (departments, ministries, leadership, etc.), but to spend some time creating the structure actually needed by the local church.

Church Growth and Church Structure

Gary McIntosh, in his book *Taking Your Church to the Next Level*,[52] reports his study of the life cycle of churches over many decades and found three key principles:

1. Unless altered by a renewal of some sort, churches go through a life cycle just like human beings: they grow, plateau, and die over a period of as many as 100 years.
2. The size of a church impacts its health and vitality because larger churches are not just bigger versions of

smaller ones but an entirely different organism, with much more complex ministries and structure.
3. *What got you here won't get you there*: one cannot lead a large church in the same way as a smaller one. In fact, what got a church to its present growth will keep it from taking the next step in growth. As the church ages and changes size, it requires new approaches to leadership, programming, training, and discipleship.

Lyle Schaller writes in *The Very Large Church*[53] (over 800) that size more than any other quality categorizes American Protestant churches. In other words, churches of different denominations and beliefs that share the same size have more in common than churches of different sizes within the same denomination. Of course, we are talking about the structure and function of the churches, not doctrine or beliefs.

As churches grow, they go through stages requiring changes in leadership and structure. Some of these changes are so radical that writers have used the word *barrier* to indicate the size of the challenge. We understand intuitively that a church of 50 cannot have the structure and leadership style of a church of 1,500. But the challenge is how to establish the structure of the church to achieve the next step in growth. People tend to be resistant to change, particularly when the things that have to change are the things that have worked in the past.

In *Overcoming Barriers to Church Growth*,[54] Mike Fletcher says, "On the road to becoming a megachurch, there are three key stages of leadership structures or configurations and two major transition points... If pastors and leaders properly anticipate these transitions and adjust appropriately, stress can be reduced and leadership teams can work together to experience growth"[55] As a pastor, Mike Fletcher took a church of 350 in Fayetteville, North Carolina, in 1985 and grew it to over 5,000 active members, at the same time developing a network of 319 churches in 43 countries. His goal in writing the book was to help churches become healthy from the inside out so that they can grow. He emphasizes that effective leadership is the key to growing a church.

He writes that churches go through two major growth barriers where the internal structure has to change radically. These changes occur around the 100/200-active-member mark and at the 700/800-member mark. Some key changes in growing beyond the first barrier is the change in role of the pastor from *shepherd* to *rancher*, where there is at least one other pastor who has the authority and respect to lead a portion of the congregation. Fletcher concludes that going through these two major growth barriers requires changes in how the senior pastor, elders, and staff relate internally, who does the ministry, and how decisions are made.

Kevin Martin[56] describes two types of growth: *congruent growth*, which happens within the current size and structure of the church, and *transformational growth*, which happens by taking the church beyond the boundaries of the current size and structure. Congruent growth occurs without having to change the structure and function of the church. In his model, this type of growth occurs, for example, as a church grows from 76 to 140 members.

Transformational growth requires a fundamental change in the church on many levels. In his model, these changes have to occur for example, when going over 140 members. He invokes sociological research to explain this "barrier," as shown next.

The Rule of 150

Malcolm Gladwell, in *The Tipping Point*,[57] a book aimed at describing corporate growth, defines less than twelve people in a group as a size in which all members can have a positive personal relationship. For example, a social group with fourteen people has ninety-two possible relationships to track. He believes that fifteen relationships is the point at which too much complexity makes close relationships difficult! Thus, twelve people in a group is a good maximum number to have in committees and on leadership boards. It is interesting to note that Jesus had twelve disciples!

Robin Dunbar, an anthropologist referenced by Kevin Martin,[58] found that the maximum number for positive relationships in a large group with one primary leader is just over 147. When studying over twenty tribal groups of primitive peoples, he found that the average size of the tribes was just over 148. He formulated the "Rule of 150," which says that at 150 and higher, the number of relationships among people becomes so complex, that the group must divide or disintegrate.

Martin believes that this rule is also applicable to churches in their growth cycle. As churches grow over 125, they become unstable because the pastor can no longer tend to the needs of the church family in a personal way as he used to do.

So how do churches grow beyond 150? The answer is to provide various social groups or small groups where people can interact. In a larger church, people create their identity by belonging to a subgroup, be it a choir, Sunday school, evangelism, or a home fellowship group. Rick Warren, author of *The Purpose Driven Church*,[59] wrote that a church can grow *larger* by growing *smaller*—using small groups to create social networks among people.

Small groups (home fellowship groups) have been effective in providing a new home for people that are breaking off their social network in the world and need to form a new one based on their faith in Jesus. But to be effective, small groups also have to be of the right size, and that is under twelve members. Beyond that number, small groups tend to lose intimacy and fall apart because they cannot provide close relationships. Various other writers such as Rick Warren, C. Peter Wagner, and Elmer Towns also agree that the key to sustained growth beyond barriers is the use of small groups where lay persons can grow in ministry, and new converts can find a home.

In conclusion, growing beyond 150 requires wise management of the interaction of groups consisting of 12 people (small groups) and 150 people (congregation-size groups). The small groups can be staff, ministry groups, or home fellowship groups. The larger congregation groups can be a church, or a subgroup of a megachurch. Understanding the interplay of these numbers will help us understand something about the growth curve of churches in their life cycle.

Local Church Structure

One of the dangers in the organization of a church is trying to do too much at once. A church that is just beginning does not need to have many departments and ministries. The key idea is to have the minimum structure to achieve the maximum impact and not burn out volunteers and staff.

In their book *Simple Church*,[60] Thom Rainer and Eric Geiger found that the healthiest churches in American tended to be *simpler;* that is, they had a simple and clear process for making disciples, and they aligned the structure and function of the church to this process. Based on their studies, they described four principles that can help a church become *simpler* and more effective:

> **Clarity**: in order to build the temple of God (the church), it is important to have a blueprint for the building process. People must be very clear about the growth process of a disciple: it must be defined, illustrated, and measured.

Movement: this is a series of steps that allows people to move from church attenders to committed servants. Each phase of the growth of the disciple is carefully planned through activities and lessons so that the believer moves from step to step.

Alignment: all activities, programs, and events of the church must be united around the process of discipleship. There must be a clear ministry process that everyone can plug into, all moving in the same direction for unity.

Focus: the church must be committed to abandoning everything that falls outside of the simple ministry process. This may mean saying "No" to some good ideas, some fashionable trends, and some traditional ways of doing church. This is a case of *less* accomplishing *more* by having a greater impact.

Let me offer a personal example. Let's start with a question: is the church a place for spiritual growth or is it a tamale stand? Putting it that way, the answer is clear. However, several years ago, feeling the pressure of fundraising, our church went into the tamale-making business. This is perfectly justified, as many churches offer all kinds of food events as a way of increasing their budget. Previously we had prepared various types of food for sale and had lunches for sale every Sunday. But selling tamales was always the most lucrative.

We had a few ladies that were skilled at making tamales, but in order to upgrade the process, I invested in a tamale-making machine from Tio Carlos' Tamale King![61] This wonderful machine can easily squeeze out dozens of tamales of various diameters with little work. To make a sad story short, Tio Carlos' machine was barely used, since the ladies preferred doing it with their hands. It was at this time that God convinced me that we were not a restaurant, but a church.

Armed with this wonderful revelation, I stood up on a Sunday morning and informed the church, to their amazement and relief, that we would no longer be making tamales or selling any kind of food. We were going to give away food if we could, and if not, we would not offer food but would focus on evangelism and discipleship. In order to make up the possible loss of income, I challenged the church to give a little more. To my delight, our income remained stable, but everyone was greatly relieved from the burden of having to make and sell food.

This is actually more according to the biblical pattern. We see in the book of Acts that the church offered food to the widows daily, and this was supported by people voluntarily giving (Acts 4:34-37; 6:1-6). I guess the Apostolic way is always better. On the other hand, if you want to burden your saints with making tamales or peanut brittle, doing car washes, or selling photo packages at Sears, that is up to you. I have done all of those, but now I prefer to focus our efforts on evangelism and discipleship, and I have found that this makes the church healthier and facilitates growth.

Church Systems

The structure of the church is a part of the systems in a church. The Bible refers to the church in various places as the body of Christ (Romans 12:5; 1 Corinthians 12:12-27). The human body has a structure, but it is not static. There are systems built around and through the structure that allow the body to function. It is the same in the church—there is a structure (organization), but it is not static, and there are systems that work around and through the structure.

Looking at churches as a combination of systems helps us to understand the work that must be done for proper functioning.

As defined earlier, *systems are cyclical patterns of behavior that accomplish a desired goal.*

Some Church Systems

Various authors have published their analyses of church systems. Rick Warren published five factors that, taken together, produce successful, growing churches.[62] These factors are based on the application of the biblical principles of the early church as shown in Acts 2. They are: Worship, Evangelism, Fellowship, Discipleship, Prayer and Ministry.

The Lawless group[63] offers a survey that will inform the church of their aptitude in each of the areas, thus opening the way for identifying the weakest factor. Jim Barber, from the Society for Church Consulting, adds other factors to Warren's 5 Scriptural characteristics, such as Resource Development (structures, stewardship), Cultural Relevance, and Church Growth Mentality.[64]

Nelson Searcy has identified eight church systems that impact the functioning of the church, and thus its growth.[65] The names of the systems are the Weekend Service, Evangelism, Assimilation, Small Groups, Ministry, Stewardship, Leadership, and Strategic.

Searcy provides seminars on improving the quality of the systems in order to achieve good health. He presents a separate focus for the Strategic and Stewardship systems, while other writers put them together under Resource Development (Barber) or Church Structures (Natural Church Development).

Pastor David Bernard in his book *Growing a Church* lists seven elements that help a church grow.[66] They are Prayer, Planning, Persistence, Preaching and Teaching, the Power of the Spirit, Personal Care (assimilation), and Personal Involvement (small groups involvement). There are many similarities between his principles and the elements mentioned by the other writers.

Natural Church Development (NCD)[67]

The NCD movement, spearheaded by C. Schwartz, is based on a study of 45,000 churches in 70 countries. The principles were discovered through a rigorous scientific study over several years that identified eight "essential qualities of healthy churches." Once these were identified, a series of surveys was developed to help churches determine which was the least effective quality (*minimum factor*). In order to be healthy, this factor was strengthened, and results were evaluated for quality and numerical growth.

The idea that focusing on the weakest step of a complex system yields increase is a principle seen in the sciences. For example, in chemistry, catalysis of the slowest step (rate-determining step) speeds up multistep reactions.[68] This principle has also been applied to business, under the title "Theory of Constraints," as developed by Goldratt.[69] In manufacturing environments, production is speeded up by identifying the slowest manufacturing step and improving it.

The NCD focus was on the quality of the eight factors, again with the understanding that improved quality would lead to growth. A 2006 revision of the original book shows that churches that applied this principle have seen a 51% increase in growth rate based mostly on conversion growth (not transfer growth).

Application of Church Systems

Regardless of which church system we may choose to apply to our church, an evaluation of the church using these ideas will help to improve the work of the church and make it more effective in reaching the lost. A few years ago, not seeing the growth that I desired, I taught the leadership of the church about the NCD systems. Although I had my own opinion, after the teaching, I asked them which of the eight systems appeared to be the weakest in our church. They unanimously identified the "Empowering Leadership system" as the weakest system in our church, to which I agreed. Following that analysis, I decided to focus on leadership development and saw positive results.

Following are simple descriptions of each of the eight quality characteristics of a growing church, according to NCD:

1. *Empowering Leadership*: leaders are called, coached, and mentored for growth. They are challenged to reproduce themselves and others in a systematic fashion.
2. *Gift-Oriented Ministry*: every believer has spiritual gifts for the building of God's kingdom. These should be identified, and each disciple should be encouraged to work in the appropriate ministry.
3. *Passionate Spirituality*: a deep and intimate personal relationship with God leads to strong convictions that are lived out with enthusiasm and joy. This attitude becomes a personal characteristic and a corporate environment.
4. *Functional Structures*: all ministries and departments should be evaluated regularly to determine how they are accomplishing their intended purpose in the church. Church structures are never *an end* in themselves, but always only *a means* to an end within the simple structure of the church.
5. *Inspiring Worship*: both personal and corporate worship should be infused with the presence of God and the movement of the Holy Spirit. During services,

there should be times of joyous celebration and also humble worship.
6. *Holistic Small Groups*: small groups are important for the growth of disciples. There, the new believer can find intimate community, practical help, and spiritual guidance. New leaders are identified and grown through leading small groups.
7. *Need-Oriented Evangelism*: evangelism should be focused on meeting the needs of the community both personally and through activities of the church. People are able to receive love from the church if they see a desire to help them in their needs. This opens the door for receiving the gospel.
8. *Loving Relationships*: genuine, practical love is at the heart of a healthy growing church. Jesus stated that the world will know that we are His disciples by our love. Real love is attractive to those outside of the church and is more effective in winning the lost that any marketing program.

Understanding church systems is a powerful way to provide direction for the growth of the church. This is not a gimmick or a quick answer, but it does provide guidance. As you read the description of the eight quality characteristics above, does one of them stand out to you as the major need in your church?

Church Systems Comparison

Study the following graphic showing a comparison of three different church systems and choose one of them for further study and application to the church you pastor. The results will be positive and powerful but understand that it will take some time to see them.

Note that these different descriptions nevertheless have similar concepts across the various systems. I have highlighted some of them in gray.

Church Health
Comparison of three published analyses of church growth factors

R. Warren /Barber / SCC*	Natural Church Development	Nelson Searcy
Worship	Empowering Leadership	Weekend Service System
Evangelism	Gift-Based Ministry	Evangelism System
Fellowship	Passionate Spirituality	Assimilation System
Discipleship	Effective Structures	Small Groups System
Prayer	Inspiring Worship Service	Ministry System
Ministry	Holistic Small Groups	Stewardship System
Resource Development*	Need-Oriented Evangelism	Leadership System
	Loving Relationship	Strategic System
		(Relationship Factor)

Common Factors

R Warren	NCD	N Searcy
Worship	Inspiring Worship	Weekend Service System
Evangelism	Need-Based Evangelism	Evangelism System
Ministry	Gift-Based Ministry	Ministry System
Discipleship	Empowering Leadership	Leadership System
Discipleship?	Holistic Small Groups	Small Groups System
Fellowship	Loving Relationship	Assimilation System-Relationship Facto
Resource Development	Effective Structures	Strategic System
Prayer	Passionate Spirituality	Relationship Factor?

*__Barber Church Consulting__ (Society for Church Consulting)
    VisionTest
        Scriptural Characteristics (Warren 5)
        Resource Development (Physical plant, Finances, Staff/Board)
        Cultural Relevance (Malphurs: social, philosophical, political, economic, technological; Percept demographics)
        Church Growth Mentality (Church Health leads to Church Growth)

Questions

1. Take a moment and draw the organizational structure of your church using paper and pencil.

2. Use some of the concepts in this chapter to evaluate the effectiveness of your structure: are there some departments or ministries that are not being effective in reaching the lost and discipling new believers? What will you do with those?

3. Look at the NCD church system model and evaluate your church. Is there one system that immediately jumps out at you as being deficient? What will you do to improve it in the next six months?

4. Use the information in this chapter as a jump-off point for further research. What can you do to learn more about church systems in your church?

Chapter 10: Key Performance Indicators for Measuring Church Health

(*Watch out for the math*)

Numbers Are Important

One of the most difficult things to do well is to use numbers to evaluate the growth of a church. From the beginning, most pastors derive much validation from the number of people that show up for services, especially for the Sunday service. Certainly, numbers are important to God, since each soul has incalculable value. But an unbalanced focus on numbers takes away from other important things, such as the health of the church and the quality of the people's relationship with God.

There are some reasons why we must use statistics wisely.

First, numbers help define reality: sometimes we think that things are one way when the reality is otherwise. Numbers help us to face the truth, even when it may be unpleasant, and they help us to face issues without blinders. Statistics can help us learn what we are doing well and what is not working. In church, people eventually vote with their feet (*i.e.*, attendance) even when they say something else out of a sense of obligation or respect to the pastor. Looking at statistics then helps everyone to understand and handle church issues appropriately.

Numbers also can help us make good decisions: strategic and programmatic decisions must be made wisely with the right information at hand. Accurate numbers help us measure the success of events and activities and provide a surer foundation than anecdotal or "feeling" types of information. This is moderated, of course, by any direction from God concerning a particular issue. The will of God always trumps any other desire or concern, and pastors must be careful to confirm His will.

Looking at church statistics also helps pastors realize the successes they are having and provides an early warning sign of possible problems. Much as a doctor looks at rising blood pressure or a team leader looks at declining sales, trends in church statistics help us identify problems before they become crises.

There are certain types of information that all churches keep. Chief among them is the attendance— the number of people that congregate at that church. And here it gets a little fuzzy. Some pastors count everybody on the church books that have attended over a certain (however defined) period of time. Other pastors report Sunday morning attendance or weekend attendance in a multiple-service environment. It really doesn't matter, so long as the numbers are consistent, clearly defined and truthful, not inflated to feed the human ego! Then, the application is to begin to see *trends* in attendance over time.

Church KPIs

Various fields use numbers to measure performance. In the medical field, physicians use *vital signs* to assess and monitor the health of patients. We are familiar with some of these, such as pulse, blood pressure, weight, and temperature. However, there are many other indicators and analyses that give the doctor more information, such as sugar or lipid levels in the blood, X-rays, MRIs, and many other tools for assessment.

Chapter 10: Key Performance Indicators for Measuring Church Health

In industry, the term KPI is used to denote *Key Performance Indicators* that help businesses assess and track the performance of the company on a regular basis. For example, in the sales field, some KPIs could be number of items sold in the month, number of active clients, inventory on hand, or number of orders. We can define seven church KPIs as follows to help the pastor and leadership assess the progress of the church.

1. Effectiveness of Church in General: *total attendance on Sundays (or weekend).*
2. Effectiveness of Evangelism: *number of first-time guests.*
3. Effectiveness of Retention/Assimilation: *number of people involved in small groups.*
4. Efforts in Evangelism: *promotional pieces distributed; new contacts made.*
5. Effectiveness in Salvation: *number of water baptisms, Holy Spirit baptisms.*
6. Effectiveness of Leadership Development: *number of members involved in leadership.*
7. Financial Strength: *number of givers and per capita giving.*

In the following pages, we will look at each of these statistics in detail. Some of these statistics can be easily calculated using a calculator (or phone). To help with all these KPI calculations, an Excel spreadsheet with these formulas built in is also available from the author if desired.

1. KPI: Church Attendance

As far as overall attendance, the most accurate and easiest number to report is the number of people present on a Sunday morning or weekend service group. The real value to the pastor is the change over time, not how it compares to other churches. If attendance numbers are up or down compared to the recent past, or last year, that gives the pastor and leadership team valuable information. I am going to call this "Sunday attendance."

Due to seasonal fluctuations in attendance, it is common to compare the Sunday attendance in a month in the current year with the same month the previous year and calculate the percentage growth (or loss). For example:

March attendance last year: 120 weekly average.
March attendance this year: 131 weekly average.
Difference: 131-120 = 11
Percent Growth = $(11/120)$ x 100% = **9%**

In this case, we can say that compared to last year, our numbers are up 9%, or we have a 9% increase. If this keeps up for the whole year and is not just a one-month change, then we can say that "our church has grown by 9% this year over last year, based on our Sunday attendance."

Now if there is *inconsistency* in the attendance pattern for the Sunday service, the church may have grown more (or less) in actual people than what is shown by the Sunday attendance. For example, for another church, we might find different numbers if we look at things as follows:

Chapter 10: Key Performance Indicators for Measuring Church Health

Last Year:
 Number of people attending all services a month: 145 average.
 Number of people attending at least three services a month: 150 average.

This Year:
 Number of people attending all services a month: 155 average
 Number of people attending at least three services a month: 169 average.

There are two ways we can evaluate our attendance growth: using the "all services" group or using the "three services" group.

"All services group:"
 Difference is 155-145 = 10
 Percent growth = $(^{10}/_{145})$ x 100% = **7%**

"Three services group:"
 Difference is 169-150 = 19
 Percent growth = $(^{19}/_{150})$ x 100% = **13%**

Thus this church may be reaching a greater number of people than before, but they are not as faithful in Sunday attendance as the group last year. This can be the case when there are many new people in church. New converts or regular guests are not as faithful in attendance as mature Christians.

It would be nice to be able to do this kind of in-depth analysis. However, it would be a challenging task to take attendance based on a roster to see how many people attend how many services in a month, etc. It is much easier to count people on

Sunday and use that number, understanding that the number of people the church is reaching may be a little different.

What constitutes a good percentage growth for a church? Some who write on this topic assert that any growth is good growth, since many mainline denominations are seeing negative growth (loss) of membership. In 2013, the greatest percentage growth of a denomination was reported by Jehovah's Witnesses as 4.37%. The Assembly of God church reported .52% growth. Several mainline organizations showed negative growth, or loss, in the same year.[70]

For any local church that desires to advance in extending the kingdom, a "good" percent growth per year is 5% based on some church experts. However, some small churches grow 15% to 30% in the early years, and some churches I am familiar with have grown over 20% per year over the first decade.

Periodically, the pastor should also assess the growth in the current year by taking the average Sunday morning attendance this year and dividing by the attendance the prior year. For example:

Last year average Sunday attendance: 123 weekly average.
Current year-to-date Sunday attendance: 142 weekly average.
Percent Growth: $(142/123) = 1.15$ - This translates to **15%** growth to date

2. KPI: First-Time Guests on Sunday (or weekend services)

The number of first-time guests that attend a weekend service is a measure of the effectiveness of evangelism. Obviously, the more guests that show up, the more effective the church has been in reaching the lost.

A good way to use this number is to calculate the percent of guests over the total attendance at the Sunday service. This

Chapter 10: Key Performance Indicators for Measuring Church Health

allows churches of different sizes and at different places in their growth curve to evaluate their effectiveness. For example:

For a small church:
    Guests this Sunday: 7
    Sunday attendance: 131
    Percent Guests: $(7/131) \times 100\% = $ **5%**

Comparing a larger church:
    Guests this Sunday: 45
    Sunday attendance: 900
    Percent Guests: $(45/900) \times 100\% = $ **5%**

Here, even though we have quite different numbers (7 vs. 45), both churches are being equally successful (5%) in reaching the lost when you consider the size of the congregation.

A good visitor percent in my opinion is around 5%, but there are no published standards on this statistic! Obviously, the higher number of guests, the more people that are going to hear the gospel, and that is good. The other side of this statistic, however, is how many guests a church can handle appropriately. In other words, how many new people is the church able to connect to through follow-up and visitation? It is also ineffective to have many guests but not be able to connect with them appropriately so that they will stay.

One good way to evaluate this number is to compare the percent of guests this month versus last month, and see what programs and activities led to a higher or lower visitor percentage.

Another way to assess the effectiveness of the church over the year to date is to calculate the guests-to-attendance ratio. First calculate how many first-time guests attend in a year. Then for example, if the average weekend attendance is 75 and the number of first-time guests is over 75, the church is doing very well, with a ratio over "1." If the ratio is below one, then greater efforts should be made so that "everyone bring one."

First-time guests year to date: 84
Average Sunday attendance: 75
Guests to Attendance= $(^{84}/_{75})$ = 1.12

The "number of guests" statistic is vital to the health and growth of the church. An often-repeated motto is "what gets measured gets repeated." Measuring the number of guests and discussing this statistic with the leadership team and the church will help the people remember that our focus is always on the harvest.

3. KPI: Retention of Guests

There is no point in having many people visit church if they walk away and don't get saved. The church needs to evaluate periodically (once a quarter, twice a year) how many first-time guests in that period are still attending church.

Based on my experience, I have discovered a simple principle concerning salvation: if a person continues coming to church, they will most likely be saved. Some Christians progress faster than others in their spiritual life, but if they continue attending church, the gospel will do its work. Thus, retention of guests is crucial to their salvation, perhaps even more than getting them quickly to baptism.

So how can retention of guests be measured? The most accurate indicator would be to review the list of first-time guests over a period of time (since the beginning of the year, for example) and determine how many are still attending church. In a small church, this task may be doable, although laborious. In a larger church, it would be more challenging. If you are in

Chapter 10: Key Performance Indicators for Measuring Church Health

a position where you can track this on a regular basis, then go ahead and keep such records. However, this is not the only way to get a handle on retention numbers.

Another way to measure retention is by counting people that develop a strong connection to the church through a small group (service group, Bible study, or cell group). The general rule is that if guests develop a good connection to the church, they are more likely to stay. For example, guests that have family or friends already in church are more likely to stay. But for them, and even more for those who don't have a friend in church, participation in a group will provide the link they need to assimilate.

A small group offers many things to a new convert. First, if they go through the painful process of losing their current friends because of their new life in Christ, they have to replace those friends. They will need the support and love of a number of people to help them make the transition. A small group provides opportunities to develop those needed friendships, and to connect through service and ministry to the vision of the church.

If a conscious effort is made to get every visitor into a small group, then the number of people participating in such groups can be a measure of the retention of guests. It is much easier to track how many people are attending small groups than to track how many guests are still attending church by the roster method. After that, the numbers are monitored for major changes or trends.

4. KPI: Efforts in Evangelism

The mission of the church is to spread the gospel, obeying the direct commandment of Jesus Christ (Mark 16:15). The number of guests measures our effectiveness, but it is also important to measure our efforts. The harder we work, the more results we will see: if we sow bountifully, we will reap bountifully.

Here each church may decide what item to measure. One simple activity that has been effective across cultures and regions is the passing out of invitations to people in public places. In the Bible, we see that Jesus and Paul often went to public places to share the gospel. Following that principle, churches can pass out invitations for church services and special activities in public places.

More traditional business marketing efforts can also succeed in promoting the church, such as mail outs by zip codes. However, the pastor must know the community and culture of his church to fine-tune what methods are effective.

The number of invitations and mail outs can become a goal of evangelism efforts, and then each month, the church can evaluate if the goal was met and what results were obtained.

5. KPI: Effectiveness in Salvation (first steps)

Following the salvation plan set forth in the gospel, we can track the number of people saved by how many were baptized and filled with the Holy Spirit. This number should be evaluated at least once per quarter as a measure of the effectiveness of the church in its mission.

The raw numbers of people baptized is probably a good way to track these activities. Then once a year or so, these numbers should be related to the size of the congregation and a comparison made to previous years. One way to do that is to determine the number of baptisms this year divided by the average Sunday attendance. There are not any known historical values for this number, but some experts place any number above 10% as a good result.

6. KPI: Effectiveness of Leadership Development

Over the course of years, the growth and health of the church are directly dependent on the number of leaders and the quality of their work. Some may call this discipleship, but to be clearer, we may further define it as the development of leaders for the harvest.

As the church grows, more and more of the work depends not on the pastor, but on other ministers and leaders in the congregation. Some of these may be paid staff, many others volunteers. In both cases, the quality of the work they do will depend on their continued growth in skills and their maturity as Christians.

Every church should have an intentional program of leadership development for both ministerial staff and for those involved in managing the church. This includes both paid employees and volunteers.

One way to measure the effectiveness of leadership development is to measure the number of people functioning in leadership positions. These are music leaders, ministry leaders, leaders of departments, paid staff, and others. Anyone that has oversight over others or is on the church staff should be considered when counting this number.

The percent of those involved in leadership divided by the Sunday attendance is one way to evaluate this. Since there are no published statistics for this number, the important issue is for the local church to evaluate the change over time. The goal would be to always have more members moving into service and leadership, since the work of the church is endless!

7. KPI: Financial Strength

One important statistic of the success of the church and its future growth is its financial status. Financial resources undergird every effort of the church, from having the proper venue to evangelism efforts.

It would be unthinkable for a pastor not to be concerned about the finances of a church. While most look at the total amount coming in, there are two other simple numbers that determine what comes in: the number of people giving and the *per capita* giving.

The number of people giving over a period time divided by the Sunday attendance is a good measure of how many are investing in the church (% givers). Additionally, the total amount coming in over a period of time divided by the number of people giving (giving *per capita*) informs the pastor of how invested the givers are in the church.

As with previous indicators, the goal is to have more givers, and for each giver to give more! Each church should establish a base line for the percent givers and for the *per capita* amount, and then monitor these numbers over time for changes to make progress in these areas.

Published Key Performance Indicators

While the focus of this section has been the tracking of an individual church's KPIs over time, there are some sources that publish statistical results for churches. These reputable sources are important in that they can provide a context to our local church statistics, gathering and publishing information about society and the religious world.

One of the most accessible reports is published by church consultants *The Unstuck Group* once a quarter.[71] This report

Chapter 10: Key Performance Indicators for Measuring Church Health

offers current church statistics on nine key areas: Attendance, Multisite Churches, Volunteer Engagement, Baptisms, Small Groups, Giving *per Capita*, Staffing Budget, Staff:Attendance ratio, Part-time Staff. This is a good resource to assess how the local church may be doing versus a wide variety of churches across the US.

Other respectable sources of church and religious statistics are the Pew Research Center[72] and the Barna Group.[73] Both of these organizations put out various reports during the year that can help inform the pastor and staff.

For more information on calculations of church growth, see appendix IV.

Questions

1. Have you been tracking the attendance numbers for your church? Look back over a few year or months—can you see any trend that is significant? Are you growing, declining, or stuck on a plateau?

2. Can you use other KPIs to increase your awareness of the health of your church? Which ones will you immediately begin to track?

3. If you feel ready, prepare a system for tracking church KPIs. Find someone that is skilled in using Excel and get them involved. Try to put in historical information and then continue forward as you learn to use numbers wisely.

4. Use the formulas in appendix IV to calculate the *average growth rate* of your church for some years.

Final Words

If you skipped over the last chapter, you are probably not the only one! Pastors are not generally known for great math and algebra skills! Just go back to it when you are ready to keep track of your great growth! Or better yet, have your son or daughter in high school read it and implement it for you ... that would be smart and much easier.

At the risk of being repetitive, I want to state again the basic premise of this book in its short form. A pastor functions as:

- A minister with anointing to help people get saved and develop as disciples.
- A leader with vision to shape the strategy and goals for the church and to motivate people to achieve those goals.
- A manager with wisdom to establish structure and develop leadership for the functioning of the church.

Learning and growing in each of these areas has helped me to grow my congregation to its present size. The principles presented here have been applied by other pastors in different means on the way to much larger churches. But somehow, even as some of them tried to communicate the story of their success to me, I missed getting it. The way I have presented it in this book makes sense to me. I hope that it will make sense to you and help you in your journey, fulfilling the calling from above.

Farewell and remember,

"God has two dwellings; one in heaven, and the other in a meek and thankful heart."
The Compleat Angler, Izaak Walton.

David Cantillo
Tampa, FL
September, 2019

Appendix I – Sample Vision Statement

Vision Statement[74]

The Northwood Community Church (Dallas, Texas): Vision is not about reality or what is. Vision is all about our dreams and aspirations or what could be. At Northwood Community Church, we envision our sharing the good news of Christ's death and resurrection with thousands of unchurched friends and people in the metroplex, many of whom accept him as Savior.

- We envision developing all our people—new believers as well as established believers—into fully functioning followers of Christ through people-friendly worship services, Sunday school, special events, and most important, small groups.

- We envision becoming a church of small groups where our people model biblical community: a safe place where we accept one another and are accepted, love and are loved, shepherd and are shepherded, encourage and are encouraged, forgive and are forgiven, and serve and are served.

- We envision helping all our people—youth as well as adults—to discover their divine designs so that they are equipped to serve Christ effectively in some ministry either within or outside our church. Our goal is that every member be a minister.

- We envision welcoming numerous members into our body who are excited about Christ, experience healing in their family relationships and marriages, and grow together in love.

- We envision our recruiting, training, and sending out many of our members as missionaries, church planters, and church workers all over the world. We also see a number of our people pursuing short-term missions service in various countries.

- We envision planting a church in America or abroad every two years.

- We envision a larger facility that will accommodate our growth and be accessible to all the metroplex. This facility will provide ample room for Sunday school, small groups, Bible study, prayer, and other meetings. While we do not believe that "bigger is better," numerical growth is a by-product of effective evangelism. Thus, we desire to grow as God prospers us and uses us to reach a lost and dying world. This is our dream—our vision about what could be!

Aubrey Malphurs
January 1997

Appendix II – MBTI Types Descriptors

| **INFJ** | **INFP** | **INTJ** | **INTP** |
| The Counselor | The Healer | The Mastermind | The Architect |

| **ISFJ** | **ISFP** | **ISTJ** | **ISTP** |
| The Protector | The Composer | The Inspector | The Craftman |

| **ENFJ** | **ENFP** | **ENTJ** | **ENTP** |
| The Teacher | The Champion | The Commander | The Visionary |

| **ESFJ** | **ESFP** | **ESTJ** | **ESTP** |
| The Provider | The Performer | The Supervisor | The Dynamo |

Appendix III – LVM for Five Choices

Line Value Model Calculation for Five Choices

Decision: what next step to take after running out of space on Sunday mornings at current location in Tampa.

- Rent larger space in a shopping center or mall for a few years
- Buy new building
- Meet in homes (GdV cell groups) without a building location on Sunday
- Multiply the congregation into several smaller groups
- Rent space weekly on Sunday morning

Chart 1: Weights of Values and Achievement of Values under Each Choice

New Building Decision		Percentage of Value Achieved				
Values	Weights (0-1)	Rent for One Year	Buy Building	GdV w/o Bldg	Plant Churches	Weekly Rental
Space for Service	1	100	100	10	100	100
Parking	1	100	100	100	100	100
Comfort	0.7	100	60	100	70	0
Access	0.6	100	100	10	70	0
Meeting Space	0.7	80	80	10	50	0
Sunday School	0.9	80	80	10	70	10
Storage	0.4	10	60	10	10	0
Community	0.9	50	50	100	100	100
Visibility	1	50	50	80	80	30
Price	1	100	20	100	50	20

Explanation:

Let's look at two items, "Space for Service" and "Storage," and see why they were given the values indicated under "Weights," and why they were assigned the "Percentage" shown under each choice.

- Space for Service: given that this was a primary goal in our move, it was given a value of 1 under "Weights" as being most important.
- Storage: since storage would be nice to have but was not too important, it was given a value of 0.4 under "Weights."

Under the Choice "Rent for One Year"

- "Space for Service" was given a 100%, since the space being considered was very large.

- "Storage" was given a 10%, since it was not necessarily a part of the rental package.

Under the Choice of "Weekly Rental"

- "Space for Service" was given a 100%, since we would not rent a place that would not have adequate space for services.
- "Storage" was given a 0%, because a facility rented on a weekend would probably not provide storage space.

Chart 2: Calculation of Choices

Multiply *Weights* in previous chart by *Percentage of Value Achieved*, then add columns down

New Building Decision		Calculation: Percentage x Weights				
Values	Weights (0-1)	Rent for One Year	Buy Building	GdV w/o Bldg	Plant Churches	Weekly Rental
Space for Service	1	100	100	10	100	100
Parking	1	100	100	100	100	100
Comfort	0.7	70	42	70	49	100
Access	0.6	60	60	6	42	0
Meeting Space	0.7	56	56	7	35	0
Sunday School	0.9	72	72	9	63	9
Storage	0.4	4	24	4	4	0
Community	0.9	45	45	90	90	90
Visibility	1	50	50	80	80	30
Price	1	100	20	100	50	20
TOTAL		**657**	**569**	**476**	**613**	**449**

Explanation:

The numbers for each choice under "Weights" and "Percentage" in Chart 1 (previous page) were multiplied together to give a new number under "Calculation: Percentage x Weights."

Examples:

Under Choice "Rent for One Year"

Space for Service:	1 x 100 = 100	The number 100 was inserted
Storage:	4 x 10 = 4	The number 4 was inserted

Under Choice "Weekly Rental"

Space for Service:	1 x 100 = 100	The number 100 was inserted
Storage:	4 x 0 = 0	The number 0 was inserted

Conclusion:

Addition of all the values under each choice scores the first choice as preferred (657).

This option might not have been the obvious one, or the discussions might have taken a long time. After guiding the group through assigning the "Weights" and the "Percentage of Values" achieved, it was easy to get to consensus with the conclusion, since we were in consensus in assigning the numbers.

Appendix IV – Historical Church Growth

Church Growth over the Years (more math)

Many pastors are interested in growth of the church in the long run. As long as this number is measured consistently (Sunday or weekend attendance, for example), it will yield results to help evaluate the growth of the church.

In the next paragraphs, I will demonstrate the math behind the calculation of the church KPIs mentioned. However, to facilitate that task, a file in the Excel format has been created with formulas already in place. To get the calculations, all that is needed is to put in the numbers for your church into the Excel file, and the calculations will be done automatically by the software. You can get a free copy of the software by contacting the author via email at "compleatpastor@gmail.com."

The first number that we can define is the percent growth over several years. Perhaps the church has been in existence for "x" number of years. What has been the yearly average growth rate (AGR) over that time?

This number is straightforward if there has been a relatively linear growth. However, we know that churches may plateau, suffer a church split, or send a group to start another church. Even considering that, the AGR gives a certain measure of the success of the church over the time measured.

The formula for calculating the AGR is the same one mathematically that banks use for calculating compound interest! By the way, this is not in the Excel sheet.

$$FA = IA(1 + AGR)^{Years}$$

Where:
  FA = Final Attendance
  IA = Initial Attendance
  AGR = percent growth (Average Growth Rate in decimal format)
  Years = number of years

Growth of Early Christianity in the Roman Empire

In a previous chapter, we referred to sociologist Stark's calculation of the average church growth for the early church from Pentecost to around 350 AD. That average growth rate was about 3.4%. That number was calculated following the same method explained here in detail.

Detailed Examples

For those wanting to work through calculations like these, let's take an example of a local church today. This church has been in existence for seven years; it began with 30 and now has an attendance of 200. What is the yearly AGR?

  FA = 200
  IA = 30
  AGR = ? (Average Growth Rate)
  Years = 7

Putting numbers into the formula, we get:

To solve this equation, one can use logs. (Remember that high school math class?)

$$\log_{10} 200 = \log_{10} 30 + 7 \log_{10} 1 + 7 \log_{10} AGR$$

Values for logs can be obtained from the calculator app in a phone.

$2.30 = 1.48 + 7(0) + 7 \log_{10} AGR$

$.82 = 7 \log_{10} AGR$

$.117 = \log_{10} AGR$

$10^{.117} = AGR$

$AGR = 1.31$

Average annual percentage growth rate is 131% for seven years, or as we would say it, the AGR is 31% per year.

Now, traditionally, this would be good growth for any church. Taking a more "reasonable" number for AGR for a church that currently has attendance of 126, what size congregation would be present in five years if the AGR is 15%?

Example:

FA = ?

IA = 126

AGR = 15% (use decimal: .15)

Years = 5 years

$FA = 126(1 + .15)^5 = 253$ (attendance in 5 years)

If this church can maintain the current growth rate, it will have attendance of 253 in five years.

These numbers don't quite measure up to numbers that might be achieved by a church using the discipleship method in a previous chapter. Many church statisticians believe that a growth rate of 5% is great because some traditional churches are in decline.

Some churches known to me personally are achieving AGRs of 15 to 20% over 10 to 20 years. I don't know of any church that is doubling every year using the discipleship method.

Your Church

Using this information, calculate the AGR for your church, writing the numbers in the table and then putting them into the equation.

FA = ____ {your avg. monthly attendance last month}

IA = ____ {avg. number of people present in your first month}

AGR = ?

Years = ____ {number of years}

$FA = IA(1 + \%AGR)^{Years}$

Calculation: put in your numbers and solve for AGR (use the *log* method as shown above)

Now calculate your projected attendance in five years if you can maintain the same AGR.

FA = ?

IA = _____ {your avg. monthly attendance last month}

AGR = _____ {number you calculated above}

Years = 5 $FA = IA(1 + \%AGR)^5$

Calculation: put in your numbers and solve for FA.

You can project attendance for any number of years simply by changing the number in the formula. But going beyond five years would be very close to guessing—anything can happen in the long run!

Tracking of Data

You can see that calculating church growth numbers is not always an easy task, but remember that you can contact me (compleatpastor@gmail.com) for the Excel spreadsheet for the church KPIs.s

Questions

1. What has been your AGR over the past few years? Are you satisfied with that? If not, what will you do to improve your growth in the next six months?

2. Do you see how church stats can help you make wise decisions for the growth of your church? List three items that you will closely evaluate using the KPIs listed in this chapter.

3. Honestly, did you just skip over this material because the math made you dizzy?

Endnotes

Chapter 1

[1] *Normal* is hard to define. For the purposes of this book, it may be defined as growth from 30-300 over the course of 5 to 10 years.

[2] Unless otherwise stated, all Bible quotes are from *The Holy Bible*, King James Version.

[3] Maxwell, John C., *The 21 Irrefutable Laws of Leadership: Follow Them and People Will Follow You.* Nashville, TN: Thomas Nelson, 2007.

[4] McIntosh, Gary, *One Size Doesn't Fit All: Bringing Out the Best in Any Size Church.* Grand Rapids, MI: Baker Books, 1999 (10th Printing, 2007).

Chapter 2

[5] Santayana, George. *The Sense of Beauty: Being the Outline of Aesthetic Theory.* C. Scribner's Sons, 1896.

[6] "For by grace are ye saved through faith; and that not of yourselves: it is the gift of God," Ephesians 2:8. And "But unto every one of us is given grace according to the measure of the gift of Christ." Ephesians 4:7

⁷ Johnston, Robin and Karen Myers, Editors. *Spiritual Disciplines*. Weldon Springs, MO: WAP, 2017.

⁸ Carrier, Steve, Verbal Bean, *The Works of the Holy Ghost*.

Chapter 3

⁹ Maxwell, John, C., *op. cit.*, 2007

¹⁰ Kouzes, James M., and Barry Z. Posner, *The Leadership Challenge*. San Francisco, CA: John Wiley & Sons, 2007.

¹¹ Malphurs, Aubrey, *Developing a Vision for Ministry in the 21st Century*. Grand Rapids, MI: Baker Books, 1999 (8th Printing, 2007), p 14.

¹² Malpurs, Aubrey, *Advanced Strategic Planning: A New Model for Church and Ministry Leaders*. Grand Rapids, MI: Baker Books, 2005, p 133.

¹³ Rainer, Thom S. and Eric Geiger, *Simple Church*. Nashville, TN: B&H Publishing Group, 2006, p 26.

¹⁴ Hyatt, Michael, *Your Best Year Ever: A 5-Step Plan for Achieving Your Most Important Goals*. Grand Rapids, MI: Baker Books, 2018.

Chapter 4

¹⁵ Katzenbach, Jon R., and Douglas K. Smith, *The Wisdom of Teams: Creating the High Performance Organization*. Bos-

ton, MA: Harvard Business Review Press, 1993.

[16] Cladis, George, *Leading the Team-Based Church*. San Francisco, CA: Jossey-Bass Publishers, 1999. Part 1.

[17] There are many resources for information on Home Fellowship Groups. See, for example:

Searcy, Nelson, and Thomas Kerrick, *Activate: An Entirely New Approach to Small Groups*. Grand Rapids, MI: Baker Books, 2018.

Gladden, Steve, *Small Groups with Purpose: How to Create Healthy Communities*. Grand Rapids, MI: Baker Books, 2011.

Neighbour, Ralph, *Where Do We Go from Here? A Guidebook for the Cell Group Church*. Houston, TX: Touch Publications, 2000.

[18] Blanchard, Ken, Patricia Zigarmi, and Drea Zigarmi, *Leadership and the One Minute Manager* (2013 edition). New York, NY: Harper Collins Publishers, Inc., 2013.

[19] For more information on the Myers Briggs personality types, visit the Myers & Briggs Foundation at www.myers-briggs.org

[20] Jamieson, Janet, and Philip Jamieson, *Ministry and Money*. Louisville, KY: Westminster John Knox Press, 2009.

[21] Dunlop, Jamie, *Budgeting for a Healthy Church*. ePub Edition, Zondervan: February 2019.

Also see Christopher, J. Clif. *Not Your Parents' Offering Plate*. Nashville, TN: Abingdon Press, 2015.

[22] Busby, Dan, Vonna Laue, Michael Martin, and John Van Drunen, *Church and Nonprofit Tax & Financial Guide*. ePub Edition. Zondervan: December 2018.

[23] Nouwen, Henri J.M., *A Spirituality of Fundraising*. Nashville, TN: Upper Room Books, 2010.

[24] The Rocket Company, *Church Fundraising Blueprint*. Seminar from www.TheRocketCompany.com. June 2016.

Chapter 5

[25] Searcy, Nelson and Jennifer Dykes Henson, *Fusion: Turning First-Time Guests into Fully Engaged Members of Your Church*. Grand Rapids, MI: Baker Books, 2017.

[26] Etheredge, Craig, *Invest in a Few*. eBook published by "Discipleship.org," 2017.

[27] Searcy, Nelson, *Why People Leave your Church*, eBook from ChurchLeaderInsights.com

[28] Pascal's Congruence Principle: "It is impossible for a person to live too long when there is incongruence between their belief and their behavior."

Chapter 6

[29] Gleason, Stan O., *Follow to Lead, the Journey of a Disciple Maker*. Weldon Spring, MO: World Aflame Press, 2016, p. 35. Following are other resources on disciple-making:

Wyrostek, Joe, *Discipleship Based Churches, How to Create and Maintain a Church of Disciples*. Chicago, IL: MPI Publishing, 2012.

Many eBook resources from www.discipleship.org, such as: *Becoming a Disciple Maker*, by Bobby Harrington and Greg Wiens, 2018. *Revisiting the Master Plan of Evangelism*, by Robert Coleman and Bobby Harrington, 2014.

[30] Stark, Rodney, *The Triumph of Christianity*. New York: NY, Harper Collins, 2011, p 156.

[31] Encyclopaedia Britannica online, (https://www.britannica.com/biography/Saint-Stephen).St. Stephen, Christian Martyr, April 10, 2019.

[32] Viola, Frank, and George Barna, *Pagan Christianity: Exploring the Roots of Our Church Practices*. Tyndale, 2012.

[33] Cantillo, David, *The Temple of God*, work in progress.

Chapter 7

[34] Malphurs, Aubrey, *Developing a Vision for Ministry in the 21st Century, op. cit.*, Chapter 1, Loc 266.

35 More information about 16PF and testing options can be obtained at: www.16PF.com.

36 Digman, J. M., "Personality Structure: Emergence of the Five Factor Model," *Annual Review of Psychology, 41,* 417-440, 1990.

37 Kessler, Steven, *The 5 Personality Patterns.* Richmond, CA: Bodhi Tree Press: 2015

38 McCrae, Robert, and Juri Allik, *The Five-Factor Model of Personality Across Cultures.* New York, NY: Springer Science + Business Media, 2002.

39 Keirsey, David, *Please Understand Me II.* Del Mar, CA: Prometheus Nemesis Book Co., 1998.

40 Jung, C. G., *Psychological Types.* London: Routledge, 1971.

41 Rath, Tom, *Strengths Finder 2.0.* New York, NY, Gallup Press, 2007.

42 Bradberry, Travis, and Jean Greves, *Emotional Intelligence 2.0.* San Diego, CA: TalentSmart, 2009.

43 Searcy, Nelson, *The Renegade Pastor's Guide to Time Management.* Church Leader Insights USA: 2017.

44 Covey, Stephen, *The 7 Habits of Highly Effective People, Infographics Edition.* FranklinCovey Co: 2015. Produced and distributed by Mango Media, Miami, FL.

Also see Hummel, Charles, *Tyranny of the Urgent.* Downers

Grove, IL: InterVarsity Press, Rev. ed., 1994.

[45] Hansen, Morten, *Great at Work: How Top Performers Do Less, Work Better and Achieve More*. New York, NY: Simon & Schuster, 2018.

Chapter 8

[46] Malphurs, *Developing a Vision for Ministry in the 21st Century*, op. cit. Chapter 5.

[47] Nee, Watchman, *The Spiritual Man*, Vol I-III. Christian Fellowship Publishers, 1968.

[48] Seligman, Martin, Peter Railton, Roy Baumeister, and Chandra Sripada, *Homo Prospectus*. New York, NY: Oxford University Press, 2016.

[49] Seligman, Martin *et. al.*, *Homo Prospectus*, ibid.

[50] Johnson, Steven, *Farsighted: How We Make the Decisions that Matter*. New York, NY: Random House, 2018.

[51] Steven Johnson, *ibid*, ascribes this phrase to Donald Rumsfeld.

Chapter 9

[52] McIntosh, Gary, *Taking Your Church to the Next Level*. Grand Rapids, MI: Baker Books, 2009.

53 Schaller, Lyle, *The Very Large Church*. Nashville, TN: Abingdon Press, 2000.

54 Fletcher, Mike, *Overcoming Barriers to Church Growth*. Bloomington, MN: Bethany House, 2006.

55 Fletcher, Mike, *ibid*, p 19.

56 Martin, Kevin, *The Myth of the 200 Barrier*. Nashville, TN: Abingdon Press: 2005.

57 Gladwell, Malcolm, *The Tipping Point: How Little Things Can Make a Big Difference*. New York, NY: Hachette Book Group: 2002.

58 Martin, Kevin, *ibid*.

59 Warren, Rick, *The Purpose Driven Church*. Grand Rapids, MI: Zondervan, 1995.

60 Rainer, Thom, and Eric Geiger, *Simple Church*. Nashville, TN: B&H Publishing, 2006.

61 By the way, I still have the Tamale King. If anyone is interested, contact me for a discounted price.

62 Warren, Rick, *The Purpose Driven Church. Op.cit.*

63 The Lawless Group, *Experienced Church Consulting for Healthy Church Results*, (www.theLawlessGroup.com). Wake Forest, NC.

64 Barber, Jim, Society for Church Consulting, (www.Barber-

ChurchConsulting.com), Andover, MN.

[65] Searcy, Nelson, *Healthy Systems, Healthy Church*, eBook, (www.ChurchLeaderInsights.com), Boca Raton, FL.

[66] Bernard, David, *Growing a Church, Seven Apostolic Principles*. Hazelwood, MO: World Aflame Press, 2001.

[67] Schwarz, Christian, *Natural Church Development*. Bloomington, MN: ChurchSmart Resources, 1996. See www.churchsmart.com

[68] Cantillo, David, this is an obvious principle to any PhD Organic Chemist like myself. Sorry.

[69] Goldratt, Eliyahu, *Theory of Constraints*. Grand Barrington, MA: North River Press, 1990.

Chapter 10

[70] Robinson, Rick, *Church Growth Rates*, from Church Growth Associates, (www.MyChurchGrowth.com).

[71] Morgan, Tony et. al., *The Unstuck Church Report*, published quarterly by www.TheUnstuckGroup.com.

Also see Morgan, Tony, *The Unstuck Church*, Nashville, TN: Harper Collins Christian Publishing, 2017.

[72] Pew Research Center on Religion & Public Life. Found at www.PewForum.org.

[73] Barna Group. Found at www.Barna.com.

[74] Malphurs, Aubrey, *Developing a Vision for Ministry in the 21st Century, op.cit.*, Appendix B.

CPSIA information can be obtained
at www.ICGtesting.com
Printed in the USA
LVHW030510200821
695646LV00001B/167